THE CHALLENGE OF
PRIESTLESS PARISHES

THE CHALLENGE OF PRIESTLESS PARISHES

Learning from Latin America

EDWARD L. CLEARY, EDITOR

WITH David T. Orique, OP

INTRODUCTION by Robert Schreiter, C.PP.S

Paulist Press
New York / Mahwah, NJ

Cover image from Digital Stock Corporation
Cover design by Sharyn Banks
Book design by Lynn Else

Library of Congress Cataloging-in-Publication Data

The challenge of priestless parishes : learning from Latin America / Edward L. Cleary, editor ; with David T. Orique, OP ; introduction by Robert Schreiter, C.PP.S.
    pages cm
  ISBN 978-0-8091-4869-1 (alk. paper) — ISBN 978-1-58768-358-9
  1. Lay ministry—Catholic Church. 2. Laity—Catholic Church. 3. Catholic Church—Latin America. I. Cleary, Edward L., editor of compilation.
  BX1920.C495 2014
  262'.1528—dc23

                         2013042430

ISBN: 978-0-8091-4869-1 (paperback)
ISBN: 978-1-58768-358-9 (e-book)

Published by Paulist Press
997 Macarthur Boulevard
Mahwah, New Jersey 07430

www.paulistpress.com

Printed and bound in the
United States of America

Contents

Editor's Acknowledgment

In his introduction to this book, Fr. Robert Schreiter kindly credits me as the person without whom the project would not likely have come to fruition. It needs to be added that Fr. David Orique, OP, has been at least as and, indeed, even more indispensable to the publication of this book. It was Fr. Orique who, shortly after arriving at Providence College from the West Coast as Fr. Ed Cleary's intended successor in the Latin American Studies Program, suddenly found himself faced with the passing of his revered mentor and, consequently, with the enormous task of sorting through Fr. Cleary's files, hard copy as well as on computer, and reconstructing the progress that had been made on his works-in-progress up to that point. He contacted the prospective contributors to this book, some of whom had already submitted their chapters, some not, and with the information at hand we decided that we were going to have sufficient material for the book to go ahead. With his knowledge of Spanish and of Latin American history and culture, Fr. Orique was indispensable to me, during the editing process, in fielding my queries and, when necessary, forwarding the queries to the individual authors. It was he and Fr. Schreiter who decided on the order of the chapters, and he who was able to provide much of the information for the "About the Contributors" section.

It is no exaggeration to say that students of Latin American religious history owe a huge debt to Fr. Orique for his unstinting work in bringing to fruition this final project of one of the most preeminent Latin American scholars of our time. I certainly owe him a huge personal debt in this regard. And I have no doubt that Fr. Ed, who has been helping us all the way with his prayers, is smiling approvingly on his dedicated protégé.

Nancy de Flon, July 2013

Introduction

Robert Schreiter, C.PP.S

THE ELECTION OF POPE FRANCIS in March of 2013 brought to the worldwide Roman Catholic Church a new focus on the Global South. Many have long opined that, since the population center of Catholicism has now shifted to the Southern Hemisphere, perspectives and priorities of the Church should be repositioned accordingly. What is becoming clear, however, is that this shift will be far more complex than many Catholics realize. In the Global North, progressives and conservatives alike tend to project their own agenda onto the burgeoning churches of Latin America, Africa, and Asia. In the wake of theologies of liberation, progressives see hope for the Global South's adopting their agenda for change in the Church. Conservatives, noting the traditional bent of many societies in the Global South, see a mirror of their own concerns and interests. The actual outcome is likely to be more complicated—even paradoxical at times.

This is just one of the reasons why *The Challenge of Priestless Parishes* will be of so much interest to a host of readers. We stand before the fact that two-thirds of Catholics live in the Global South, but two-thirds of Catholic priests reside in the Global North. How are we to read this phenomenon? How are we to analyze its origins and development? And what are we to make of it? Is it a problem that

1

needs to be addressed? Or is it an opportunity to reset the whole picture and ask fundamental questions about priesthood, the sacraments, the laity, and engagement in the Church altogether?

This book about the absence of priests in parts of Latin America is a response to different aspects of this problematic. Christianity has been in Latin America for half a millennium and has been the majority religion there as well. For more than half that time, it was sponsored by and protected by the state. It went through turbulent challenges in the nineteenth and twentieth centuries, with the challenges coming from different sides. Throughout that time, it had a ratio of priests to people that was very high, but even the gap that such figures represented belied the further fact that priests were often concentrated in the urban areas, leaving the rural regions without almost any priestly presence whatsoever. What the analyses in this book offer in looking at a church without priests may not be paradigmatic for other parts of the world, but they do represent a careful and thoughtful set of studies that could encourage similar efforts to look at this problematic elsewhere.

The first chapter, by Edward Cleary, OP, sets the stage and the tone for what follows. He investigates the challenge the Church in Puerto Rico faced after the Spanish-American War in 1898. Spanish priests who had been serving the island largely left for Spain, leaving a priestly vacuum. In the rural areas, which had never been fully served, lay men (and then women) stepped into the void as preachers. Known as Hermanos Cheos, they built chapels where people could gather, pray together, and hear doctrine expounded by the Hermanos. This built on the tradition of the *rezadores* and *rezadoras*, or pray-ers, present in rural areas. It was not intended as an alternative to the institutional Church, but rather as an expression of people's religion in the absence of a more clericalized form. Cleary makes two important points that help us view a Church without priests in the entire region. First of all, the top-down parish approach to ministry, which only became universal in the Church after the Council of Trent, assumes that the people come to the priests. What is being suggested here in the ministry of the Hermanos is that the priests should come to the people. The chapels that were built were the forerunners of the base Christian communities that were to emerge several decades later. Second, Cleary invites us to consider more than one way of being Catholic. This does not dismiss or disregard Roman Catholicism; rather, it invites us to see the contextual character of Roman Catholicism, with its strengths and its limitations, and to be prepared to imagine other faithful forms of being Catholic that are less clerical in nature. As the world Church continues to unfold, we need to keep this prospect before us.

Cynthia Folquer, OP, expands our perspective to look at the indigenous cultural and religious base with which Catholicism had to interact. She focuses her attention on indigenous peoples in northwestern Argentina. There she notes the historical encounter with the *conquistadores* and relates how indigenous people received the Catholicism offered them. This is an important contribution because the indigenous foundation upon which Christianity was built in Latin America has remained very strong throughout the continent wherever indigenous ways have been able to sustain themselves. The way indigenous religion integrated its own concerns—about religion, about health, and about environment—offers insights for the fragmented, hyperdifferentiated world in which postmodern people now live. She pays special attention to ways in which women were the carriers and transmitters of faith, and how they have maintained Christian faith and practice over generations. Here again, we can gain insight into how to live out our faith in Christ in a way that does not require so many clergy.

Bruce Calder widens our perspective in yet another manner. From the perspective of Guatemala, he traces the history of the development of the Church from the colonial period up to the present time. He cites the devotional practices and lay associations of the Ladino classes, derived largely from Spain. Alongside this, the majority Mayan population integrated Christianity into their indigenous traditions. He introduces and expands upon the influences coming from Europe in the first half of the twentieth century—Catholic Action, the Cursillo Movement, and new methodologies for a Christian engagement with the world. These were to have a profound effect throughout the continent. The see-judge-act methods of reflection found among the Young Christian Worker and the Young Christian Student movements laid the basis for modes of reflection in the base Christian communities and the theology of liberation of the second half of the twentieth century. It provided a new way for lay Catholics to engage their faith beyond the popular religion forged out of the encounter of Iberian Catholicism and indigenous traditions. The Charismatic Renewal is the final element to be added into the historical mix. This movement, which resembles the Pentecostalism that is now grown large in many parts of Latin America, has often been seen as the polar opposite of the theology of liberation. Calder does us a great service by pointing out some of their common roots and what these two together portend for the future of Catholicism in the region. The empowerment of lay people in all of these movements give us yet another dimension to the picture of what a Church without (or with fewer) priests can mean in a positive dimension.

Brian Pierce, OP, gives an example of a bishop-initiated process that responded to having few priests. This was the "Delegates of the Word," who would gather people on Sunday for prayer and reflection on the Scriptures. The "delegates" were delegates of the bishop. Somewhat different

4

from the Hermanos Cheos we had seen earlier, this was something initiated by and guided and developed by the bishop. The Hermanos were never in opposition to the bishop, but had sprung up independently and came to work with the bishops. Pierce's example explores not only the origins of the delegates, but also how the bishop accompanied them in the political conflicts that marked so much of Central America in the 1970s and 1980s. This shows what can be entailed not only in initiating responses to the problematic of a Church without priests, but also what is involved in sustaining them.

Nadir Rodriguez da Silva, OP, reminds us at the outset that having lots of priests does not guarantee the vitality of a local church. Her perspective comes from northeastern Brazil, which has long suffered from a paucity of priests like so many other areas of Latin America. In her contribution, she chronicles how initiatives were taken by lay Catholics to build up and sustain a vital life of faith, even sometimes in the face of opposition from the clergy. Her chronicle helps reassert that while the Eucharist is the central sacrament for Catholics, it is baptism that is foundational. Here the teaching of the Second Vatican Council on the importance of baptism and seeing the Church as the people of God comes fully into its own.

In a concluding chapter, David Orique, OP, brings together the insights of the various authors in an extremely helpful way. After charting the history of Christianity in Latin America and the different social and political factors that have played significant roles in that history, he goes on to draw out what can be learned from Latin American experiences of being a Church without priests. He notes, following Cleary, that there are different expressions of Catholicism, and that these have to be taken into account in addressing the problematic. Not all expressions of faith happen in the church building. The role of home-based

Catholicism, of smaller gatherings to share faith and reflect together on the Scriptures, cannot be overlooked. He goes on to examine common factors found in all the contributions to this volume: the importance of inculturation processes, the significance of primary relationships, the major roles of women and youth, and the growing awareness of lay responsibility. The Church is more than buildings and bishops. When we address a Church without priests, we need to keep that perspective in mind.

The project that has resulted in this book was conceived and developed by Father Edward Cleary, OP, one of the preeminent scholars of the Church in Latin America in our time. A passionate and congenial scholar, there have been few who can match his knowledge of the Church in that part of the world. In 2009, he contacted me about writing the conclusion to the book, to which I agreed. On November 21, 2011, Ed died unexpectedly. In the intervening time, the manuscripts he had received and the correspondence he had had with the authors needed to be reconstructed. Paulist Press editor Nancy de Flon kept with the project persistently. Without her, it is likely that it could not have come to fruition. In 2012, Ed's colleague and confrere, David Orique, OP, graciously agreed to join us in completing the project. He offered many helpful insights into the material in this book, as well as writing a synthetic conclusion to the book. The central province of the Dominican Friars in the United States, of which Ed was a member, was also very helpful in assisting in the project. In this new configuration, I took on writing the introduction and David Orique wrote the conclusion. It is the hope of all of us that this book will be a suitable memorial to the life and work of one of the great scholars of the Church in Latin America.

Palm Sunday, 2013

1

Puerto Rico:
Lay Preachers Who
Preserved Catholicism

Edward L. Cleary, OP

THE SHORTAGE OF CATHOLIC CLERGY has become the major preoccupation of the Catholic Church in the United States and Europe. No end to the crisis is in sight. Although it has not been commonly recognized, the Catholic Church in Latin America has already faced priest shortages in modern history. Despite these grave deficits, the Latin American Church has emerged into the twenty-first century with a considerably enlarged workforce of priests and sisters, and polls have shown that the level of public confidence in the Church is the hightest of any institution in Latin America.

How the Church survived in long periods without clergy forms the central focus of this book. Of all the lands in which priests have been scarce or nonexistent, few can match Puerto Rico in the way the organization and dispersal of the Hermanos Cheos addressed the situation. Their development into a coherent and effective movement came only gradually and with very little support from the official Catholic Church. In fact, at the beginning of the twentieth century, only a handful of middle-level pastors and administrators saw considerable value in laymen assuming preaching and teaching roles, which typically had been reserved to priests or to well-trained laity who had been approved by the Church.

Hermanos Cheos ("Brothers Joe" in English) came about because of abrupt change in government in Puerto Rico, which brought a great vacuum to an already struggling Catholic Church. When the United States declared war on Spain and its army invaded Puerto Rico in 1898, large numbers of priests began leaving the island. They were, for the most part, Spanish and were dependent on the Spanish government for their salaries and for financial assistance to maintain aging church buildings.

Church and state had been unified in Spain and Spanish territories, as well as in some countries in Northern Europe, in the 1800s. This meant that the state-supported church received not only financial support but also an assured place in society that gave state churches privileges and a large degree of protection from competition from other religious contenders. In some countries, such as Sweden, this protection was extreme. Roman Catholics and some other Christian denominations were forbidden to own property or to conduct religious services. Puerto Rico's Catholics had almost the same degree of protection from competitors under late nineteenth-century Spanish rule.

But Spain's ability to keep out religious outsiders was wavering and its financial support of the church was meager, for many reasons, including the Spanish state's overly stretched financial abilities to cover salaries and church upkeep at home and in the colonies. Further, Puerto Rico had few economic resources to offer Spain and almost no clout in increasing Spain's subsidy over the centuries. In a word, Puerto Rico was a poor possession. It never offered an abundance of gold, silver, or other natural resources that the favored colonies provided. Human resources, including priests from Europe, flowed toward the main seats of

Spanish rule. Political power, education, and large human settlements were established elsewhere, in such places as Lima, Antigua (Guatemala), and Mexico City. Puerto Rico was a backwater province of the Spanish empire, and its state church reflected that quality. In the 1890s, it was a ramshackle institution on a largely impoverished island. Its clergy were not Spain's most talented or ambitious.[1] As noted by the North American bishop who took over after most Spanish priests left, there was profound hatred for the church because the Spanish priests were presumed to be hand in glove with Spain and against the people.[2] Moreover, Spanish clergy were insufficient for the pastoral care of the island's Catholics. Puerto Rico's mountainous topology and its few and dangerous roads meant that thousands of rural or isolated parishioners seldom saw a priest. The Spanish colonial church's territory was stretched beyond its resources.

The greatest Church poverty of all was its relative lack of native clergy (and religious sisters) after four centuries of the presence of Catholicism on the island. At the time of the Spanish defeat in 1898, only thirty-four of the 137 diocesan or religious priests were Puerto Rican.[3] It was, in terms of religious professionals, a foreign church, a fact that was further emphasized when clergy and religious sisters from the United States gradually filled in for the departing Spanish bishop, priests, and sisters.[4] At a low point in this transition, only thirty-four of the eighty-six parishes on the island were attended by clergy, and of these some were barely taken care of.[5] The Spanish did not provide adequate care for the island's Catholics in remote or scattered settlements.

The first North American bishop of Puerto Rico, the German-born naturalized American from New Orleans, Bishop William Blenk, worked extremely hard to reconstruct the church in Puerto Rico, but he reported after the first five years that as far as he could see, "the power of the church to do good has been destroyed."[6]

Where Puerto Ricans were in control of the practice of Catholicism was in the domain of popular religion. In place of a Catholicism centered on a church as a place of worship and a gathering place for a community of believers who took spiritual, moral, and physical care of one another, a different kind of Catholicism had grown up. Popular religion as practiced by these Puerto Ricans meant religion practiced by and typically passed on from the women of the families, primarily mothers or mother substitutes. Home altars, memorized prayers, rituals of praise and petition, and devotion to the saints were hallmarks of this religion. This religion, also called folk religion, contrasted to what is called official, or orthodox, religion refined by academic theology and largely practiced by literate and educated Catholics.

Popular religion as practiced in Puerto Rico at the end of the nineteenth century and beginning of the twentieth century was especially centered in recitation of the rosary.[7] This devotion, which originated in the late medieval period and was promoted especially by Dominican preachers in Europe and later in colonial territories, emphasized the principal "mysteries" (divine interventions) of Catholicism from the birth of Jesus to his death and resurrection. As with most popular religious devotions, its practitioners modified it to fit their own limited understanding of Catholicism. The rosary in the hands of some Catholics was a Marian devotion and, for the spiritual greedy among them, an instrument for bargaining with the Mother of God to seek favors from her son.

This understanding is the polar opposite of that of the celebrated author Garry Wills, the Northwestern University professor of classics and history, who explained his views in his 2005 book *The Rosary*.[8] If Wills' interpretation is correct, the rosary was an effort of lay people to have their own extended prayer. They wished to have something similar to the Divine Office used by monks, friars, priests, and deacons.[9] It certainly served that purpose in Puerto Rico. The rosary was incorporated into rural life on the island long before the Hermanos Cheos came into existence. Because the celebration of Mass was so infrequently available to them, rural Puerto Ricans used the communal recitation of the rosary in place of the Mass.

The practice of saying the rosary was especially centered in praying for the recently deceased. Rosaries were said on nine successive days after death; three rosaries would be prayed at the wake or on the ninth day after death; three rosaries would be said on the yearly anniversary of the death for seven years.[10] Puerto Rican Catholics also prayed the rosary on the occasion of special crises, such as approaching hurricanes, or on main feast days. (The Hermanos themselves anchored their lives through praying the rosary three times a day— morning, noon, and night—and often persuaded others to join in with them.)

The rosary was thus part of neighborhood or village life and the heads of households invited neighbors, friends, and families to join in. These informal get-togethers were ready made for the Hermanos Cheos, who would join in the reunions and at the end of the recitation of the rosary, ask permission to speak. They then preached so effectively that they acquired a wide reputation for being holy persons or wise persons. They were frequently invited back for another evening or to another house in a chain of invitations.

Environment That Brought
Cheos to Preaching

In the eyes of Puerto Ricans, the taking over of the country by the United States was a foreboding event. Puerto

Ricans did not know what to expect, nor was the United States fully clear in its policies and intentions about language, culture, and religion. For a time, it appeared that Puerto Rico was to become an extension of the United States and no longer a Spanish-language and Spanish-culture country. The main indicator of that intention was language: English, supplanting Spanish. Public education was to be largely conducted in the language of the conquerors and the teaching of the Catholic faith excluded.[11] Moreover, as the Protestant historian Samuel Silva noted, a new system of public education was allied with the Protestant missionary movement. The U.S. official overseeing education reminded the Protestant minister Victor Clark, educational commissioner in Puerto Rico, that "education which contemplates a change of the native language implies a change of religion and a complete change in the body of a people's traditions."[12]

Puerto Ricans expected that just as the Spanish state imposed Catholicism, the North American state would impose Protestantism on the Puerto Rican nation.[13] In terms of religion, Puerto Ricans believed they were faced with an invasion of Protestants who would aggressively seek to make Catholics into Protestants. This impression was reinforced as Protestant denominations from the USA divided the island up into territories, giving several groups a certain priority in proselytizing a specified territory. This type of agreement, called a comity agreement, was common among Protestant missionary groups in the twentieth century and was intended to avoid unnecessary competition among groups that had limited resources.[14] For Catholic Puerto Ricans ignorant of such history—Protestants, after all, only really became missionary in the early twentieth century—it seemed like conquerors dividing up the spoils. Further, some, if not most, Protestant missions of the type that came to the Caribbean and Central America at that time emphasized the building of structures. Be they churches, schools, orphanages, or hospitals, these structures reinforced Catholic Puerto Ricans' perception that foreigners were intent on putting roots down and taking over.

This perception was especially strong in the remote areas of Puerto Rico. In the cities and towns, the dominance of Catholicism in religion had been diminished by anticlerical Masonic lodges, religious indifference often common to urban life, and the increased presence of foreigners from other religions. In Ponce, the largest city at this time, the city council was controlled by freethinking anticlericals.

Protestants were making inroads before 1898. From the 1860s, Protestants from Great Britain, Germany, and the United States came to Puerto Rico as immigrants and visitors who lived largely within foreign enclaves where Protestants practiced surreptitiously. Political turmoil in Spain and interest in European liberalism in Puerto Rico allowed for partial but important openings to other religions. Some Protestant groups, such as Anglicans, were allowed to conduct public services at Ponce as early as 1873.[15] (They could hold services but they could not toll the church bells.)

Before surveyors drove the first sticks in the ground for marking out new Protestant churches and schools in Puerto Rico after the North American conquest, lay Catholic men and women began to face up to the threat of their families abandoning the Catholic Church. They began a grassroots counteroffensive in the most remote areas of the island. The most important of these efforts was the movement of the Hermanos Cheos. How they arose and carried out their mission constitute the main themes here.

Spontaneous Response from Lay Preachers to Crisis

For a variety of reasons, including the semiliterate character of the first members of the Hermanos Cheos and the mystical language used by historical narrators, the early character of the brotherhood needs careful interpretation. What is recounted here follows the narrative generally accepted by Puerto Rican historians.[16] The two founders of the lay movement were both called José. Hence in Puerto Rico, where the plural of José is often Cheo or Cheos, the two men and their followers were called Hermanos Cheos (Brothers Joe).[17]

The first lay preacher named José was José de los Santos Morales Rodríguez, who was born into a farm family in the northern coast city of Arecibo. At twelve years old, he felt called by God to dedicate his life to God and the Church in some fashion that was not yet clear to him. He felt his faith in God threatened by the influx of Protestants to the country. That year, 1898, the Americans invaded the island and he heard that they were going to promote Protestant beliefs and attack Catholics, ridiculing their religious practices, especially the saying of the rosary and the use of religious statues and pictures.

This vision of impending threats grew, and Rodríguez became increasingly concerned that his fellow Christians were poorly educated in Catholic beliefs. Historian Esteban Santaella quoted him as saying: "I wish to organize an army of peasants to defend our faith and devotion to the Blessed Virgin."[18] Although, like many Puerto Ricans at the time, he was barely able to read or write, he began preaching in 1902, four years after the North American invasion, to whomever would listen.

This occasion has been regarded as the founding date for the establishment of the Hermanos Cheos. At the age of sixteen, José Morales began his preaching in his own neighborhood, Arrozales of Arecibo. No one offered him money or other support to start this ministry. He acted on his own to enter into the religious struggle that he perceived as bombarding and troubling his neighbors. His main message was that of maintaining the Catholic faith through a life nourished by the sacraments: confession, taking communion, and going to Sunday Mass to hear the preaching of priests.

José Morales set out from Arecibo as an itinerant preacher to the small settlements found in the mountainous central portion of the island. In contrast to the mainland United States, where isolated peoples lived on the western frontier, Puerto Rico had its remote and isolated settlements in the mountainous center of the island. The distances to these settlements were not great but the terrain was broken and rocky. The primitive paths were tortuous.

During these journeys José Morales encountered José Rodríguez Molina at Adjuntas. In José Rodriguez, Morales met another strong personality whose traits complemented Morales's impetuosity, and the two Josés had a working agreement to share what leadership might be needed in their new venture.

The small town of Adjuntas, on the western slopes of the central mountain range where coffee growing had been a thriving industry, was populated by a number of Italian-French immigrants from Corsica. In 1898 the town was buffeted by a great hurricane and suffered extensive damage that required years of rebuilding. That same year, Yankee troops invaded the island and established a military base at Adjuntas. In these circumstances, driven by the same compulsions as José de los Santos Morales, José Rodríguez Molina decided at age twenty-three to dedicate himself to lay preaching.

José Rodríguez was also marginally educated, slightly adept at reading and writing, and was taught the basics of the Catholic faith by his mother. The key moment in his early life occurred while he was in another small town, Utuardo, east of Adjuntas, where the feast of the Magi (Epiphany) was being celebrated among several hundred persons at a private residence. After the rosary had been prayed, José asked the owner of the house and property if he could say a few words (a euphemism for preaching) to those assembled. This was the first time he preached publicly. He continued preaching missions for most of the rest of his life, some fifty-five years. One of his main contributions was the alliance with José de los Santos Morales. Together they gave shape to the movement of lay preachers. They thus had a strong hand in the reconstruction of the Catholic Church in the rural areas.

About 1902, in the nearby mountain town of Ciales, two other Puerto Rican Catholic men wanted to become home missionaries. Vicente Aviles González and Juan González met up with José de los Santos Morales and agreed that the latter would act as director of their preaching band and that they would use Ciales and the town of Florida to the north as the bases of their preaching. At a date no one is certain about during this early period, three Hermanos and one Hermana met and voted that José Morales be president of the new group. This was called El Pacto Cheo (the Cheo Agreement), the basic oral legal agreement that served thereafter as the foundation of the brotherhood.

The legal and formal organizational aspects of the brotherhood derive from this Pacto. It was understood that there would be an elected president of the group to whom the members owed basic obedience, but that the president would consult with members. Yearly assemblies eventually became common. While the members elected the president, for some years this was understood as an office that continued for life—terminated by death, renunciation, or resignation. This was later modified to three-year terms, allowing for successive re-elective terms.

At the beginning, it was understood that José Morales would be president for life. He continued in office until 1939.[19] In the first two decades of the Hermanos, José Morales and his cofounder, José Rodríguez, added some of the best Cheo preachers. Morales increasingly spent time in Ponce, then a city larger than San Juan, and less time in the countryside. José Rodríguez based his activities from 1907 in Barrio Guayaguao, also in Ponce. Rodríguez needed to live in an urban environment for the education of his ten children.

What was most striking among the first lay preachers was the spontaneous quality of their vocations. They decided on their own that some kind of reaction was needed to head off the Protestant threat and fill in for the missing priests. The Cheos were not clergy wannabes. They were still very much laity. At first, these preachers engaged in their missions as single persons, but most of them married and remained members of the missionary group. The two Josés who were the cofounders were notably dedicated to their wives. Generally speaking, the Hermanos had married persons as their predominant sector. During the first eighty years, the presidents of the group, all elected within the group, were, with one exception, married men.[20] The election of a single person, in the 1970s, was considered a failed experiment.

One of the historical milestones of the congregation was the marriage of a Cheo and a Chea. Hermano Pedro Laboy married Hermana María Lamberty in 1910 and became the second president of the congregation when José Morales died. It is noteworthy that of the seven children from this marriage, the first son, Ernestino, became a priest. In addition, Father Laboy later became spiritual director of the Cheos.

Hermano Pedro Laboy joined in the lay mission work after viewing the work of the Cheos. He trailed along as an apprentice with José Rodríguez and Hermana Geña on their missionary trips through the mountains. When Laboy asked about joining the brotherhood, Rodríguez consulted with José Morales. In 1907 both agreed that Rodriguez would act as master teacher and mentor to Laboy. At first Laboy was entrusted with teaching simple catechism lessons. In 1908 he was allowed to preach on his own at a chapel with which he was entrusted. José Rodríguez continued, largely from a distance, to monitor the ministry of Laboy, who was not yet fully approved by the Cheos. The approval process involved interviews, observation, and a lengthy *prueba* (practicum) by the main *jefe*, José Morales. He was thereafter authorized by Morales to preach in any place on the island.

Women as Chea Preachers

Not a great deal is known about the circumstances in which Hermana María Lamberty, the wife of Hermano Laboy, began preaching, except that she began at an early age in the early 1900s. She likely started preaching not long after José Morales took up brief residence in her home town of Utuardo, affected by his example. That a woman would take up preaching in the Catholic Church at that time was a remarkable ministry and probably would have been protested and blocked in most places in the world. In Puerto Rico at that time, preaching by women was not considered an issue.[21] Before and after marriage, Pedro and María took turns preaching, one following after the other at the podium. They apparently preached as equals and gender was not noted as a problem raised by their listeners.

After the marriage, the couple was assigned to the chapel at Quebradillas as their base. They bought a small farm near the chapel to provide food for the family.

Hermana Maria continued in her normal ministry until the seven children demanded more of her time at home. But, while remaining at home, she continued to preach and to catechize at the Quebradillas chapel and nearby areas while Hermano Pedro went all over the island. Maria would put a baby in a bassinet and carry the child to the chapel or wherever she would be preaching in nearby hamlets.[22]

Hermana María was not the only woman preacher. The best known Chea was Eugenia Torres Soto, better known as Hermana Geña. She was born on a farm in open country near the western city of Mayaguez. At the time of her birth, her parents were not very religious, and they waited until she was thirteen before having her baptized. She was barely educated, having attended fourth grade while living with extended family in Guayamillas. While there she went with her mother to see and hear what was widely publicized by word of mouth as the local appearance of "The Man of God," Hermano José Morales. His preaching, she believed, converted her to a life dedicated to God. Not long after this experience of hearing and talking with Morales, while Geña recited the rosary with others, she felt an impulse for the first time to preach after the rosary. She was of an indeterminate age, between eleven and thirteen years old.[23] From that time on, she continued preaching, encouraged by family and neighbors.

Her father insisted that she needed to be acknowledged as a preacher by the Cheos, so she and her mother had to make seven trips (of almost a week each time) walking from her home in Runcio before they were able to catch up with José Morales at his base of operations at Peñuelas. Each time, they were hosted graciously by Hermana Michaela Reyes, the first wife of Hermano Morales and herself an effective preacher. Hermano José heard Geña preach three times and approved of what he heard. He wrote a letter to the patroness of the chapel at Geña's home chapel at Runcio, saying that he recognized and recommended her as a Chea preacher.

A year later, Hermano Morales thought Hermana Geña would do better away from her home territory and assigned her to Barrio Real de Ponce. Because she was an only child and still very young, her mother felt obliged to stay with her. At Barrio Real the Catholic faithful rented a house and supported mother and daughter financially (proving that preachers do not have to depend on government subsidies, as the departing Spanish had believed). Later her father sold a parcel of land and went to Real, where he bought a plot of land and built a house for the family. She and her parents moved every few years, generally receiving a cordial welcome, except for the Redemptorist Fathers at Barrio Borinquen, Caguas. She described them as "muy ariscos" (surly) with her.[24]

Two years after her mother died, she married. The three principal leaders of the Cheos—Brothers Morales, Rodríguez, and Leboy—told her to stop preaching. (Apparently they disapproved of her husband.) She stopped preaching but acted as sacristan, did a little pastoral counseling, and helped out at a chapel attended by the Vincentian Fathers. She did not have a happy marriage, separated from her husband, lived as a single mother for ten years, and gave her two children to the care of an orphanage so that she could return to preaching. After much deliberation within the Cheos, she was formally rehabilitated as a Chea preacher in 1938 by José Morales with the approval from the spiritual director, Father Noell. She returned to preaching with notable success, especially preaching along with the Hermanos Cheos at their retreat house at Peñuelas. But she was gradually worn down by age and died at age eighty-three in 1974.

The bishop of Ponce, Fremiot Torres Oliver, who knew Hermana Geña well, conducted her funeral and praised her values and virtues. At that time, hers was only the second burial of a Cheo or Chea conducted by a bishop. Two months before she died, the Hermanos Cheos at their annual Assembly reversed an earlier decision and approved entry of women into the congregation, opening the door again, they hoped, to women of Geña's competence and success.

Itinerant Preaching and the
Reach of the Movement

From 1902, this folk religious movement spread its influence over most of the southern and central parts of the island and toward the east and the sugar plantations. Preachers concentrated their efforts in the mountainous coffee-growing central sections from Penuelas to San Lorenzo and from Ponce to Corozal. This movement was a response from the grassroots to the institutional crisis of the Church. The Church, as noted, did not have a deep grounding in the people because of Spanish ecclesiastical incapacities in the colonies.

But this lay initiative in religion was not entirely new. In the mountains at the end of the nineteenth century there was a tradition of lay "pray-ers" (*rezadores*—persons devoted to praying), male preachers, and female preachers. One of the most famous of lay preachers was a woman whom people called the Saint of the Mountain or Nuestra Madre Elenita. She was from San Lorenzo but had a wide influence in the Caguas region. Elenita and others sustained interest in Catholicism that the Hermanos Cheos were able to cultivate.[25]

Chapels and Communities as Key Institutions

From their beginning, Hermanos Cheos built small chapels. José Morales began preaching in 1902. By 1913, eleven years later, the Cheos had thirty chapels. The motive for these chapels, historian Esteban Santaella stated, was the need for large covered spaces. The shacks in which small farmers lived had no space for holding prayer meetings or preaching sessions. The only large dwellings were on the few large haciendas owned by large landowners. The *hacendados* were not always friendly to the Cheos and could not be counted on to volunteer their plantation-style houses for Cheos preaching. Preaching in the open air was not an option because of the tropical sun or frequent rain at certain seasons of the year.

From the beginning, then, the Hermanos, who were thought of as otherworldly itinerant mystics, members of a messianic movement, were in fact highly practical builders of key structures for anchoring the practice of faith in the countryside. The chapels were much more than shelters from the torrid sun or rain; they became the centers for basic catechesis and preaching among the increased following the brothers had attracted. With so few priests available, the Hermanos hoped to draw priests at least once a year to celebrate Mass at the chapel on the feast of the patron saint of the chapel. Priests, Santaella wrote, were impressed with the Cheos' work of drawing people together who were not able to go to urban parishes. The patronal feast then became an occasion for celebrating Mass and administering the sacraments.

In effect, these chapels filled in the spaces between parishes, which existed mostly in cities and towns. The parish has been a feature of Christianity for more than a thousand years, and the need for it is taken for granted. It is the basic unit of the Catholic Church, and by ever-increasing legislation in church law over the centuries it became the place for recording basic membership and for participation in the sacraments.[26]

The basic weakness of the parish as administered by many priests was the presumption that parishioners would come to them rather than the minister going to where the people resided. The yearly visit of parish priests to the countryside for patronal feasts offered only transitory pastoral attention.

Chapels, then, increased the reach of parishes. Most of all, the chapels were gathering places of small communities. One of the typical patterns for the pastoral care of community members was the assignment of a Hermano(a) as preacher to a particular chapel. (Some preachers were assigned only to preach in a particular place, while others ranged widely while maintaining their home near a particular chapel.) Typically this chapel assignment meant obtaining a plot of land near the chapel to build a house for the preacher and family, who would then farm the small plot. Proximity to the chapel also indicated integration of the preacher (and family) within the life of the community. Their house and the farm were usually similar to those of the neighbors: wooden shacks with thatched roofs and enough crops and fruit trees for subsistence.

The preacher and family lived like the others, among them, dependent on the same fate of crops and weather. Their preaching thus emerged from a shared environment of the grassroots. There was a community of life among neighbors and a community of belief. It was unusual in the Catholic Church that the word of God was preached from such a deep bond of shared lives within a living lay community—a situation not unknown, however, in earlier church history.[27]

One can see in the small chapels and their communities the precursors of a great innovation of the Latin American Catholic Church in the twentieth century, the base Christian community.[28] (Variations of the same innovation include small church communities throughout the world and home churches in Cuba.) Small groups came together on a regular basis to pray and to hear the word of God preached to them, typically followed by shared reflec-

tion or questions and answers. The high point of their calendar to which they looked forward was the celebration of
the Mass and the administration of the other sacraments by
a visiting priest. But their gathering together constituted
them as church. The gathering, rather than worshiping as
solitary persons, was essential because when the baptized
gather for worship, they are church, not the whole church
but a cell within a living body of the church. The group
members believed that the biblical promise of "Where two
or more are gathered in my name, there I will be," was ful-
filled for them.

These Christian base communities grew out of a shortage of clergy in Latin America. "The goal of small communities," wrote the Latin American scholar Daniel Levine,
"was to provide small-scale, familiar, and accessible envi-
ronments in which people could meet" for prayer and reflection. In addition, Levine noted, the communities offered a
place for access to sacred knowledge through catechesis and
preaching.[29]

Further pastoral motives led to the creation of the
chapel system. From the viewpoint of effective preaching,
the Cheos believed they needed formal and stable centers.
Previously they acted spontaneously with emphasis on situ-
ational preaching—for example, at funerals or other family
and community gatherings. (This was roughly similar to the
early Christians' use of homes for worship.) Now they
wanted a space for worship and catechesis of their own, an
environment clearly dedicated to religion and one that they
could use when they wished.

Further, the efforts of walking strenuously as itinerant
preachers was heroic. But Morales had been on the road for
years, and the effort took a toll on him and on others who
matched his time on the road. They could also see that effective preaching about faith and values requires much more
time than short-term residence allows. Morever, the Hermanos

and Hermanas had grown to a group large enough to effectively have a division of labor by territory. The first chapel was constructed at Veguitas, Jayuya and was moved to Puerto Plata, Jayuya, where a shrine setting, called a throne, was also constructed for an image of St. John the Evangelist, patron of the Hermanos. The chapel was destroyed by a hurricane, rebuilt, and placed in the care of Hermano Magdeleno Vásquez.

In addition to the social and theological dimensions of the chapel communities, the economics of the situation were important. It cost money for land, land titles, construction materials, repair and rebuilding after hurricanes, and upkeep. The issue was: Who pays for preaching and for religion? The European model followed by the Spanish, Portuguese, and French in the Americas had been to expect the state or the rich to provide for upkeep of churches and clergy. Many Spanish clergy left the island when state support stopped. Spanish priests who lingered in Puerto Rico after the North American invasion found themselves in deep poverty. Church officials attempted measures to sustain them, such as imposition of set fees (*aranceles*) for services rendered; a certain number of U.S. dollars for baptisms, for example. This did not work well, but people at the grassroots were not asked for their opinions.

In contrast to the colonial-style Spanish church, the faithful did supply money and other resources to support Cheos preachers and their dependents. They also furnished the resources (land and titles, construction costs) needed for the chapels. No money from the institutional church, as far as is known, went to support the Cheos or the chapels. The very poor gave what they could in food or other donations. Those who had a surplus—the lower-class entrepreneurial types or semi-professional persons, such as shopkeepers, traders, or tradesmen—were asked to be patrons or sponsors. Many of the chapels had a person or a couple named as the *mecanas*, sponsors, looking after the chapel while a Cheo was said to be "directing" the chapel.

The sponsor of the chapel and the community frequently rented or built a house for the preacher and supplied food. Some preachers had received contributions from the faithful that enabled them to buy property and build their own homes, ones that tended to be simple and unadorned, at least in the early decades. Morever, at the beginning of the movement the preachers often moved to other assigned places while the sponsors remained in place. The community had a stable abode; the preacher often did not. To a considerable extent, the preacher was the servant, not the master of the community. This was the direct opposite of the European organizational model of the church in force at the time. In many ways, the Cheos helped change the attitudes of a major sector of Puerto Rican people about economic support for the church, at least in the central and southern regions. Decades later, Bishop James Edward McManus of Ponce would tell his priests that they would be dying of hunger if it had not been for the Hermanos Cheos who taught the faithful to contribute alms to the Church.

The Cheos chapel model was not a parallel universe without priests; the high points of chapel life were the visits of priests for Mass and other sacraments. Preaching and catechism lessons given during ordinary times were pitched toward that Mass and the sacraments. In a word, Mass and the sacraments administered by priests were held up as essentials of Catholicism by the Cheos. As a minimum, the priestly visit occurred once a year on the feast day of the patron saint of the chapel. This date was fixed in the universal church's liturgical calendar and would be known by both resident community and itinerant preachers. The choice of saint as the patron saint of a specific chapel was varied in order to avoid an overlapping of celebrations. Thus the available priest or priests could visit a variety of chapels rather than having to choose among many places with chapels named San José or Santa María. Puerto Ricans love celebrations, so patron saint feasts were joyous and memorable events.[30] The visiting priest at the center of these celebrations was treated as a king, someone special. He was not an outsider at these events; he was there by right, a right reinforced by the preaching of José Morales and the other Cheos.

What took place in the chapel during ordinary time (as contrasted to patron-saint fiesta time) was catechism lessons, recitation of the rosary, and preaching. The rosary anchored the prayer lives of the Cheos. It was to be said three times a day, morning, noon, and evening. Members of the chapel community were invited to join in. Catechism lessons, called by Puerto Ricans of that time *dar doctrina*, were a recitation of the main dogmas and doctrines of the Catholic faith. This knowledge was fundamental to both preacher and audience. And the practice of teaching doctrine and dogma was clear evidence of the Cheos' desire to teach respect for orthodox Catholicism.

The genius of the Cheos was the use of popular religion to turn it toward orthodox religion and practice. While secular and Protestant commentators on Puerto Rican religion saw the Cheos as perfect embodiments of the "superstitions" of folk Catholicism (especially, in their view, the hated practices of honoring Mary and the saints),[31] José Morales and the Cheos clearly directed instruction and preaching toward basic truths of Catholicism and toward the sacraments. Devotions to Mary, the saints, and the rosary were ways to arrive at these goals.[32]

Moreover, their pastoral practices found strong vindication in recent papal teaching. Referring to popular piety as "the soul and precious treasure of the peoples of Latin America," Benedict XVI urged pastors to promote and protect the popular expressions of the faith of the people since

27

"these are an authentic expression of our Catholic faith."[33] Contrary to Catholics who seemed Protestant or Calvinistic in their practices, the Latin American bishops at Aparecida taught that popular religiosity is a valid spirituality.[34] This spirituality is especially to be honored since it is the spirituality of the poor, the neglected, and the excluded, the kinds of persons reached by the Cheos. Popular religion can and should be purified through Scriptures, sacraments, Eucharist, and service to others, as also emphasized by the Hermanos.

Vast cultural differences between the United States and Latin America existed. Latin American culture and religion was born out of European and indigenous cultures. Mainline U.S. culture was born and shaped out of Calvinism and other strains of European religions, without extensive interchange with the indigenous cultures of America, and U.S. Catholics have been deeply influenced by that Calvinist culture.[35] The Cheos and their listeners showed clearly that Puerto Ricans chose to continue Latin American Catholicism. In other words, there is more than one Catholicism. Early twentieth-century Puerto Rican or Spanish colonial Catholicism[36] was a distinct Catholicism, a form of Christianity as distinct as Greek Orthodox Christianity is from that practiced in the ancient Orthodox churches of Syria and Persia.

By 1933 Hermanos Cheos had forty-four chapels in rural areas and had brought together thousands of peasants to renew their faith, abandon concubinage, assume within their daily lives religious practices, and attend Mass. Samuel Silva Gotay believes that their evangelizing zeal matched that of the Protestant preachers in the mountains, keeping these regions Catholic after the invasion of 1898. Thus the Hermanos Cheos acted as bulwarks against Protestants, sweeping great numbers of Puerto Ricans who were largely ignorant of Catholic teachings into their folds.

The Cheos also helped to keep alive what can be described as Latin American mysticism. That mystical spirit continues and is very much alive in Puerto Rico. Reinaldo Román, a professor of history at the University of Georgia, wrote of present-day Puerto Rico as "a country where sanctuaries and pilgrimage sites are found nearly on every corner of the map; where talk of apparitions and miracles and the supernatural figure almost daily in talk shows, newspapers, and casual conversation; and where preachers mobilize followers by the tens of thousands to gather them yearly before the capitol."[37]

Issue of Authenticity

The Hermanos Cheos preached, recruited, and organized a distinct group of lay Catholic preachers. Not every interested person was invited in and some were suspended as members. They had no special religious preparation beyond the traditional devotional practices of faith learned at home and the limited catechesis made available by missionaries to the isolated rural communities through four centuries of Spanish colonial history. They were, for the most part, illiterate men and women who preached with a great evangelical and moralizing fervor. They took their inspiration from John the Evangelist. He became their patron to the extent that peasants who listened to their preaching thought of the Cheos as almost reincarnations of the apostle.

Once the two Josés organized the Cheos, preachers had to be recognized and certified as authentic members. This formal recognition was not a question of schooling and credentials but of being vetted, that is, of having one's beliefs, preaching, and lifestyle evaluated by José Morales. In this way the Cheos were often called "Los Eligidos" (The Select Ones) to indicate that they had been selected by José Morales or someone assigned by Morales to examine the novice preacher.[38]

The control of who preached as a Cheo was more strictly exercised than many observers imagined. The Cheos were thought to be freelance entrepreneurial types who took to preaching on the spur of the moment and did so without anybody's "by-your-leave." But Hermano Morales was an active supervisor who permanently suspended five notable preachers, including Antonio and Gregorio Rodríguez, blood brothers who were among the first companions of Morales. Gregorio later created his own group and continued preaching. Antonio obeyed and stopped preaching, as did the other three who were suspended. The issues for suspensions seem not to have dealt with orthodoxy of doctrine but with failure to accept new assignments.

Discernment of the authentic Catholic character of preachers on the part of the peasant audience was a delicate issue. The remote areas of the mountains and other regions of the island were visited by a variety of itinerants, including various kinds of preachers, politicians, and ideologues. The Cheos were far from being the only lay Catholics who were preaching at this time. Gregorio Rodríguez, as noted, was suspended from preaching as a Cheo but continued preaching and enlisted other preachers to join him. In some places, such as Junco, José Morales had been so eloquent in his preaching that several lay men at that place took up preaching on their own, not joining the Cheos.

For a family or a community visited by one of these itinerants, it was difficult to judge whether the stranger who showed up on their doorstep or asked permission to preach after the family rosary was Catholic, Protestant, promoter of the Partido Unionista, or a rogue mystic. Father Esteban Santaella recounts that when he was a child, a man showed up at his family's farmhouse, claiming to be an Hermano Cheo. Santaella's father extended a cordial greeting but went off to check on whether the stranger was indeed a Cheo. The stranger was not allowed to preach in their community that evening.[39] The stranger remained a guest with the family for three days. On the third day, when Señor Santaella left home to attend the recitation of the rosary for a newly deceased neighbor, the stranger went with him and was allowed by the deceased's family to preach after the rosary. The preacher's language seemed to be more political than religious; he used such terms as "Latin America" that were not common in Puerto Rican peasant circles. The next day the stranger disappeared and was not seen again.

What was at work, theologians would say, was a *sensus fidelium*. The baptized have the gift of the Holy Spirit that allows them to judge whether the message being preached is the word of God that demands their assent or whether the message is not the word of God.

The Cheos were, for the most part, *jíbaros*, peasant farmers.[40] The rural language they used was simple and rough-hewn but effective for an illiterate audience. The faithful needed to be called to a message of hope, since they lived, said Samuel Silva, in a world of supernatural histories, superstitions, and fantasies, submerged in poverty and underdevelopment, vulnerable to violence and recklessness, as described by the novelists and essay writers of the period. Many of the remembrances of the surviving Hermanos were written in the poetic language of peasants. This included apocalyptic prophecies.

Relations with the Institutional Church

The few priests serving Puerto Rico in the early twentieth century were mostly located at some distance from the rural areas covered by the Brothers and a few Sisters in their itinerant preaching journeys. What the priests in this first period knew of Hermanos Cheos was largely by word of mouth. One set of these reports was highly favorable. The Brothers, people said, were commonly called *Los Inspirados* (the Inspired Ones), *Los Santos* (The Holy Ones), *Los Enviados* (The Ones Who Were Sent), *Los Predicadores* (The Preachers), and many similar phrases.

In contrast, one of the first reactions published in 1906 from Ponce was strongly negative. A Catholic periodical from there said that "the origin of these inspired ones is (Afro) spiritist....These angels are diabolical."[41] In his "Notes for the History of the Missions in Puerto Rico," a pastor from Ponce, then the largest city on the island, wrote in 1909: "These 'Inspired Ones' [were] 'spiritists, crazy, or fanatics.'" Nonetheless, he noted that despite the many foolish things they said, they should be acknowledged for keeping the poor farmers out of Protestant hands, promoting religious marriage, Catholic baptism, confession, and communion. "Without doubt these preachers should be credited with the extraordinary number of Catholic marriages and baptisms."[42]

The gradual development of a shrine center at Jayuya led to a closer relationship with the institutional church. The Cheos also recognized their own physical limitations of going out to individuals and groups as itinerant preachers in the difficult environment of the mountains, so they also attracted people to come to them in pilgrimage at a central place, Jayuya, where they built a chapel. Thousands would journey there, especially for the major feast. (By one account some fifty thousand pilgrims would make the journey to the shrine at the high point of its popularity.) The Hermanos needed a priest for the centerpiece celebration of the Mass.

By the time the shrine was being planned, a North American bishop had taken over from his Spanish predecessor. In 1913 José de los Santos Morales, as president of the Brothers, wrote to the bishop, William Jones, to establish formal ties with the institutional church. He wrote that when the chapel was completed they hoped to name it in honor of St. Philip the Apostle, invited the bishop to bless the chapel, and petitioned that the Capuchin Fathers, a branch of the Franciscan Order, from the parish of Utuado be appointed to be the chaplains of the pilgrim's chapel, thereby beginning the formalization of the Cheos' relations with the institutional church.

This chapel would be a place where they could carry on oral catechesis and where a Catholic priest would celebrate Mass. In his short and direct letter to the bishop, Morales made clear that the Hermanos had constructed the chapel at San Lorenzo Heights, Jayuya, "to combat falsehood and root out from the human heart the errors of Protestantism, spiritism, freemasonry, and whatever else is not in conformity with the Catholic Church." Previously Bishop Jones had not condemned the Cheos but was practicing "watch and wait" in dealing with the unusual movement. In his response to Hermano Morales, he granted authorization for the priests from Utuado to serve at the chapel, sent his blessing, but declined to bless the new chapel himself.

This was not the end of the questioning about the movement. Two years later, in 1915, as mandated by Rome, the bishop ordered an investigation of the Cheos. The pastor of Utuado, the Capuchin friar Manuel José de Palacios, wrote a formal response recommending the Cheos. They were, he said, "true Catholics, who were always ready to submit to obedience" and "frequented the sacraments." He considered their moral conduct "laudable" and exemplary in the sense that they contributed to the moral uplift of the peasants. They contributed to the lessening of concubinage and their influence kept Protestants and spiritists from taking hold in the *barrios*. Opposition to the Cheos, he wrote, occurred because of their uncultured peasant language and lack of technical theological discourse.[43]

The Spanish Capuchins furnished the first spiritual director for the Hermanos, Fray Angel de Lieres. He was asked by José Morales to be the first spiritual director of the

Cheos. For some time, he based his preaching at the Brothers' central pilgrimage chapel at Jayuya. Despite Fray Angel's good intentions, his other pastoral obligations prevented him from offering consistent spiritual direction.

Final approval of the Cheos as a group was still lacking. In 1918 the results of the bishop's secretary's investigation of the orthodoxy of the Hermanos went to Rome by means of the Apostolic Delegate (the Vatican's representative to Puerto Rico), Monsignor Trocchi. The Apostolic Delegate went to Jayuya to see for himself what the Brothers were doing. His visit occurred as some ten thousand pilgrims were present at Jayuya. A Capuchin missionary, Fray Estanislao, recounting many years later his experiences with the Hermanos, said that the Delegate, seeing the great religious fervor of the Brothers' followers, including the partaking of the sacraments, was pleased with what he witnessed. After imparting his blessing, the Delegate recommended that the Brothers not begin their preaching by invoking the name of their patron saint since this, he said, confused their listeners. He also said, "I will say to the Holy Father that you are loyal sons of the Catholic Church. I also recommend to you that you become Third Order members of the Franciscans."[44] In response to the Delegate's report, Pope Benedict XV sent back his approval of their activities.[45] Their legal status as a movement or association was yet to be determined.

The bishop's secretary was key in the approval of the Hermanos as a congregation, their increased incorporation within the Church as institution, and their theological and spiritual orientation. Father Gonzalo Noell, who had grown up at Bayamón near San Juan, received theological training both in Puerto Rico and the United States. This allowed him to be a linguistic and theological bridge between the American bishop and the presumably strange (to American eyes) lay preaching group.[46]

Twenty years had passed since the Hermanos had been

organized by José Morales, but they had no consistent spiritual director. In Padre Noell, they found the person they wanted as spiritual director and chose him. In the narrative of this occurrence by the historian Father Santaella, it was noteworthy that the Brothers chose their spiritual director (an act of relative autonomy) rather than having a spiritual director imposed on them in an authoritarian fashion. It was a wise choice in many ways, as Noell apparently led an exemplary priestly life (in contrast to priests mentioned by Bishop Blenk, Puerto Rico's first bishop, priests whose unfaithfulness had been causes for scandal).[47]

Further, the Brothers gained an incomparable *patrón* when Noell was named the number two administrator of the diocese of Ponce. (Patrons within the Catholic Church have been at times indispensable defenders of religious orders and movements.) When the new see was created at Ponce in 1924, Noell became vicar general, the highest-ranking Puerto Rican in the diocese. He remained in that post for many years, while also assuming the pastorate of an important parish with the city. Although his title of Monsignor meant little more than an honorary membership in the papal household, it did indicate his status as a person of influence in the diocese and the larger church. From then on the Hermanos had stability in their spiritual direction by priests and in their relations with the church.

The larger question that might have been raised about lay persons preaching was not a stumbling block in the recognition of the valuable role of the Brothers. However, the lack of training was increasingly addressed through the addition of theological courses to the preparation of the new entrants.

In 1919, Fray Estanislao, as superior of the Capuchins who were working pastorally with the Brothers at Jayuya, was asked by the bishop about the legal status of the Brothers in the Church. He responded that he did not believe that their joining the Franciscan Third Order would be best but recommended that they be granted canonical status as a lay movement in the Church that would be called the Congregación de San Juan Evangelista.

The Puerto Rican Church was reorganizing itself at the time. While the departing Spanish bishop and clergy would have known the history of relations of the Brothers to the Church, the newly arriving North American bishops and priests knew little of the origins of the Brothers, and this delayed a decision about the Hermanos.

In 1924 Ponce became a new diocese as a result of that reorganization. The first three bishops of the diocese were *gringos* (North American born and bred) who held office for thirty-nine years, between 1924 and 1963. This change of cultural leadership could have brought drastic changes but instead brought consolidation of the Brothers within the church. In 1927 the North American bishop, Edwin B. Byrne, canonically established the Brothers as the Roman Catholic Apostolic Association of St. John the Evangelist and assigned a priest as spiritual director. Byrne was succeeded by two mainland bishops and then by Puerto Ricans who were promoted to be the residential bishops of Ponce, beginning in 1964. Throughout the changes, the institutional church in Ponce continued to support the presence and activity of the Brothers.

While the Apostolic Association of St. John the Evangelist had a loose organizational charter and no religious vows, it did have stability of leadership in its initial years, with José Morales continuing as president from 1903 until his death in 1939. Further, Morales exercised a strong hand in the selection and preparation of new candidates. He had increased time for administrative oversight after he stopped preaching in 1912. No one knows for certain why he stopped. Santaella speculated that it could have been a self-imposed penance or one imposed by an ecclesiastical authority. For some time, he continued to go on the road, with two Hermanos Cheos to do his preaching.[48]

Decline and Evaluation

By the 1930s, the Hermanos were at a critical time in their history. From the beginning of their work, the brothers were convinced that they had a special vocation or charism: that the Cheo missionary ought to arise spontaneously from among the people. By the middle of the third decade of the 1900s, the flow of vocations was drying up. Brother José Morales had suffered so many tests and disappointments that he was reluctant to receive new vocations into the brotherhood. During this period in the early 1920s, he made a promising aspirant, Brother Carlos, wait nine years before admitting him to the congregation. Female entrants were barred completely, with Hermana Geña being the last accepted.[49]

By 1933 the Hermanos had declined almost to oblivion. Only five brothers remained and most were physically unable to be fully active. Three of the remaining brothers ventured out on missions three or four times a year. The quarter of a century of itinerant preaching, hard travel, and fighting to hold things together took their toll. But, more significantly, José Morales could see that the parishes on the island had an increased contingent of clergy and new lay movements with numerous members. The congregation was not as necessary for preserving the Catholic faith in Puerto Rico.[50] Some speculated that the decline of the Hermanos Cheos began some time earlier when the Hermanos went to live in towns and cities. But larger, economic forces were at work bringing about the disintegration of Puerto Rican agrarian society.[51] By the 1930s, this process had greatly reduced coffee and sugar production. The days of splendid feast days at Jayuya were over, but the religious vitality of

Puerto Ricans in the twentieth- and twenty-first centuries was far from extinguished.[52] The Hermanos Cheos continued on in Puerto Rico in altered fashion, a history that is too long to recount here.[53]

José Morales died in 1939 and his funeral was well attended, although it was not celebrated as a national event. He died as he lived: poor, leaving only his second wife (he remarried after the death of his first wife), a small house, and a farm plot. He had given his life to God and the Church, it was believed, out of profound love, despite the incomprehension and calumnies he faced.

The early pioneer lay preachers died or their lives faded out in retirement, leaving the impression that the time of the Brothers was over. Reinaldo Román wrote in 1999 that the itinerant Cheos preachers "disappeared" from the main venue of their activity, the mountainous coffee country. This occurred, he wrote, "with little sense of loss among the new American Catholic hierarchy."[54]

"We are faced," wrote Samuel Silva Gotay, the preeminent (and Protestant) religious historian of Puerto Rico, "with a vast rural movement of poor lay persons, the majority of whom were illiterate, who took into their own hands the preaching of the Gospel with the intent of facilitating the conversion and the moral reconstruction of open countryside and urban poor neighborhoods of Puerto Rico, especially those places where a priest never or very seldom visited."[55]

By 1933 Hermanos Cheos had forty-four chapels in rural areas and had brought together thousands of peasants to renew their faith, abandon concubinage, assume religious practices within their daily lives, and attend Mass. Silva Gotay believed that their evangelizing zeal matched that of the Protestant preachers in the mountains, keeping these regions Catholic after the invasion of 1898.

What was most distinctive about the Hermanos Cheos

as lay persons was their assumption of responsibility for preaching and for shepherding the faithful toward the orthodox practice of Catholicism. If the twentieth century was a new age of the laity in the Catholic Church, the Hermanos Cheos were among the pioneers.

NOTES

1. Samuel Silva Gotay, "The Ideological Dimensions of Popular Religiosity and Cultural Identity in Puerto Rico," in *An Enduring Flame: Studies on Latino Popular Religiosity*, ed. Antonio Stevens Arroyo and Ana Maria Diaz-Stevens (New York: Bildner Center for Western Hemisphere Studies, 1994), 136.

2. Samuel Silva Gotay, *Catolicismo y política en Puerto Rico: Bajo España y Estados Unidos; Siglos XIX y XX* (San Juan: Editorial de la Universidad de Puerto Rico, 2005), especially 313–22 (The reference here is from 240). Silva Gotay's works also reflected wide scholarship through his organization of a large working group called the Equipo Inter Universitario de Historia y Sociología del Protestantismo y Catolicismo en Puerto Rico.

3. Ibid.

4. Not all replacements were North American. Several Spanish groups remained or returned to the island. Dutch Dominicans supplied new leadership in place of the Spanish Dominicans.

5. Silva Gotay, *Catolicismo y política en Puerto Rico*, 241.

6. Joseph Blenk, "Report on the Diocese of Puerto Rico," June 5, 1905 ASV SS Fascicolo 550, fl 20–55. Copies in English and Italian.

7. Among scholarly treatments of Puerto Rican popular religion, see Stevens-Arroyo and Díaz-Stevens, *An Enduring Flame*.

8. Garry Wills, *The Rosary* (New York: Viking, 2005).

9. Ibid., 3.

10. Three rosaries at that time meant the commemoration of three sets of mysteries, the joyful, sorrowful, and glorious, each devoted to five mysteries.

11. Language policies have varied through the years, beginning with English as the main instrument of public education until 1915, modified again in 1937 under President Roosevelt toward more complete instruction in English and later de-emphasized.

12. Silva Gotay, "Ideological Dimensions of Popular Religiosity," 140–41.

13. Bishop William Blenk, quoted by Silva Gotay, *Catolicismo y política en Puerto Rico*, 238.

14. Nine groups shared in the Comity Agreement; they included Presbyterians, Methodists, Baptists, Congregationalists, and Disciples of Christ.

15. Luis Martínez-Fernández, *Protestantism and Political Conflict in the Nineteenth-Century Hispanic Caribbean* (New Brunswick, NJ: Rutgers University Press, 2002), passim.

16. Esteban Santaella Rivera, *Historia de los Hermanos Cheos: Recopilación de Escritos y Relatos* (Santo Domingo: Editors Alfa y Omega, 1979; 2nd ed., 2003); José Dimas Soberal, "Los Hermanos Cheos," paper presented at Encuentro Nacional de la Sociología del Catolicismo en Puerto Rico, University of Puerto Rico, 1997; Lillian Rodríguez Pérez, "La obra de los Hermanos Cheos" (master's thesis, Centro de Estudios Avanzados de Puerto Rico y del Caribe, San Juan, 1994); see also Samuel Silva Gotay, *Catolicismo y política en Puerto Rico*, and Reinaldo Roman, *Governing Spirits: Religion, Miracles, and Spectacles in Cuba and Puerto Rico, 1898–1956* (Chapel Hill: University of North Carolina Press, 2007), esp. chapter 2.

17. Caribbean Spanish speakers frequently drop the final "s" in both speech and writing of the plural form; hence both Cheo and Cheos have been used in Puerto Rico.

18. Santaella, *Historia de los Hermanos Cheos*, 61.

19. Ibid., 107.

20. The first single person elected president was Carmelo Vásquez Vásquez. He was elected in 1963 and

reelected for another three-year term. A year after finishing in that office, he married. Father Santaella wrote that thereafter "the experiment with celibate brothers [as president] was terminated"; he does not explain further.

21. The history of women as preachers in the Puerto Rican Catholic Church is far from comprehensive.

22. The Leboys continued in Quebradillas until 1933, when they moved to Ponce for the formal education of the children.

23. Rural people at this time in Latin America often did not know (or think it important to know) their exact age.

24. Santaella, *Historia de los Hermanos Cheos*, 156.

25. For Elenita and other precursors see Rodríguez Pérez, "La obra de los Hermanos Cheos," and Román, *Governing*.

26. Parish records included information on parentage, baptism, confirmation, marriage and clerical ordination, and Christian burial. It did not include frequency of participation and typically did not note generosity.

27. The Benedictine abbeys at certain periods in their history were closely tied to agrarian communities.

28. Scholarly and popular literature on the communities is vast. For a summary statement see Daniel H. Levine, "Base Communities," in *The Encyclopedia of Politics and Religion*, ed. Robert Wuthnow (Washington: Congressional Quarterly Press, 1998), 1:69–71. See also Frei Betto, "What Is the Base Ecclesial Community," in *Latin American Religions: Histories and Documents in Context*, ed. Anna L. Peterson and Manuel Vásquez (New York: New York University Press, 2008), 221–26.

29. Levine, "Base Communities," 69.

30. Epiphany especially is celebrated in southern Puerto Rico as a highly staged multi-day event. The Puerto Rican government spent more than $900,000 in Epiphany gifts to children in 2009.

31. Nélida Agosto Citrón, *Religión y cambio social en Puerto Rico, 1898–1940* (Río Piedras, Puerto Rico: Ediciones Huracán, 1996), passim, esp. 80–81 where the followers of

the Cheos are characterized as plagued by magical-religious notions.

32. A small but important body of research by Puerto Ricans on *religiosidad popular* has grown up since the 1990s. See especially Angel Quintero Rivera, ed., *Virgines, magos, y escapularios: Imagineria, ethnicidad popular en Puerto Rico* (Rio Piedras, Puerto Rico: Centro de Investigaciones, Universidad de Puerto Rico, 1999) and the multi-volume works edited by Anthony Stevens Arroyo and others for the Bildner Center Series on Religion.

33. Benedict XVI, quoted by the Latin American bishops, *Concluding Document*, Fifth General Conference of the Bishops of Latin America and the Caribbean, Aparecida, Brazil, May 13–31, 2007. No. 258.

34. Ibid., Nos. 258–65.

35. Virgilio Elizondo, "Aparecida and Hispanics of the U.SA.," in *Aparecida: Quo Vadis?*, ed. Robert Pelton (Scranton, PA: University of Scranton Press, 2008), 57–70.

36. See the argument for the continuation of the colonial church in twentieth-century Puerto Rico in Elisa Julián de Nieves, *The Catholic Church in Colonial Puerto Rico (1898–1964)* (Río Piedras: Editorial Edil, 1982), with epilogue for the 1970s.

37. Reinaldo Román, review of Nélida Agosto Citrón's *Religión y cambio social en Puerto Rico, 1898–1940* in *Journal of Social History* 32, no. 3 (Spring 1999): 711.

38. Santaella, *Historia de los Hermanos Cheos*, 43.

39. Ibid., 44.

40. *Jíbaros* are commemorated by prominent statutes in eastern Puerto Rico.

41. *El Ideal Católico*, August 4, 1906.

42. For a more complete view of clergy-Cheo relations, see Santaella, *Historia de los Hermanos Cheos*, 169–90.

43. Santaella, *Historia de los Hermanos Cheos*, 180–84.

44. Estanislao Peridiello, *La misión en Venezuelsa, Puerto Rico y Cuba: Cuarenta años de apostolado de los capuchinos de la provincia de Castilla* (Caracas: Tipografía Americana, 1930), 119.

45. In 1903 Pope Leo XIII separated ecclesiastical jurisdiction of Puerto Rico from the church province of Cuba and placed Puerto Rico directly under the Holy See.

46. Nélida Agosto Cintrón stressed the anti-popular religion sentiments of U.S. missionaries to Puerto Rico who removed numerous saints' images in Catholic churches and chapels in *Religión*, 87–88.

47. Blenk, "Report," 20–55.

48. Santaella, *Historia de los Hermanos Cheos*, 90.

49. See Silva Gotay, *Catolicismo y política en Puerto Rico*, 454–57, for his argument about the non-alliance of Hermanos Cheos with anti-American political forces.

50. Santaella, *Historia de los Hermanos Cheos*, 94.

51. Comprehensive views of the sweeping changes can be found in César J. Ayala and Rafael Bernabe, *Puerto Rico in the American Century: A History since 1898* (Chapel Hill, NC: University of North Carolina Press, 2007) and James Dietz, *Economic History of Puerto Rico: Institutional Change and Capitalist Development* (Princeton, NJ: Princeton University Press, 1986).

52. Protestant and Catholic Pentecostalism, the latter also named the Catholic Charismatic Renewal, would sweep through the island. See also Ana María Díaz-Stevens and Anthony Stevens-Arroyo, *Recognizing the Latino Resurgence in U.S. Religion* (Boulder, CO: Westview, 1998).

53. In 2009 the Cheos president, Arturo Ramos Ruiz, reported one hundred active brothers and forty members in formation (Interview, Peñuelas, July 30, 2009).

54. Román, review of Nélida Agosto Citrón's *Religión y cambio social en Puerto Rico, 1989–1940*, 711.

55. Silva Gotay, *Catolicismo y política en Puerto Rico*, 317.

2

Argentina:
Praying Women Ministers
and Keepers of the Faith

Cynthia Folquer, OP

THE HIGH MOUNTAIN INDIGENOUS communities of
northwest Argentina have maintained a strong tradition of
Andean Christianity without benefit of resident priests for
centuries. How they accomplished that only became evident
after twenty years of observation. I found evidence of the
effects of the first evangelization of Christianity mixed with
indigenous religiosity. Jesus Christ and the Virgin live har-
moniously with the earth goddess Pachamama, nature goddess Llastay, and several deities of nature.

When priests are scarce—as they have been for centuries in this region of Argentina—indigenous communities
have maintained their version of Christian religiosity
through a deeply embedded cultural system in which lay
persons assumed responsibility for the practice of faith.
Women have been especially active as ministers who pray
and educate children in religion.

There is clearly a mixture of Catholic tradition and
ancestral religion. Through the years of my friendship with
and investigation of these communities, I discovered that it
was women who kept alive the memory of the native and

45

Catholic traditions. I recorded their voices, prayers, stories, and songs as part of an oral history analysis. In this chapter, I will address how women acted as the custodians and teachers of tradition to preserve the faith for centuries with only the sporadic presence of priests.

The high mountain region in Tucumán is a severely isolated area, even in such a modern country as Argentina. The region is so far removed from highways that it can be reached only on horseback along the countless paths that crisscross mountains and gorges. Several places that I investigated are six to eight hours away from tiny points on the map—for example, Raco and El Siambón, to which I traveled by bus or car and then switched to horseback. (Riding horses is a long-standing skill for Argentine men and women.) A few landing strips for small planes are located in hamlets and are typically used only for medical emergencies.

The indigenous communities studied are in the districts of Trancas, Tafí del Valle, and Tafí Viejo of Tucumán province. They have had electricity from solar panels for only four years. They can now watch television and thus they have more contact with urban life.

The Sporadic Presence of Priests

Evangelization in this region began in the middle of the sixteenth century, when the first priests came with the conquistadors. The presence of priests was always scarce in Tucumán, which is some distance away from Buenos Aires, and very sporadic, particularly in the mountainous regions. No statistics of priests are extant for earlier historical periods for this province, but table 1 shows the prolonged scarcity of priests.

Date	Source	Population in Tucumán	Priests
	Table 1.		
	Priests and Population of Tucumán Province[1]		
1869	National Census	108,953	55
1914	National Census/ Ad Limina Inform	332,933	88
1949	Ad Limina Inform	659,117	149
1961	Ecclesiastical Yearbook	742,000	155
1972	Church Annual Statistics	559,307[2]	139
1981	Church Annual Statistics	703,708	127
1992	Church Annual Statistics	815,075	111
2000	Church Annual Statistics	996,178	132
2008	Church Annual Statistics	1,158,870	149

From the colonial period, this region of the Southern Cone was a marginal area of the Spanish Empire. Hence it was only infrequently that a bishop came to administer the sacrament of orders. The few candidates for the priesthood typically had to go to Buenos Aires, Córdoba, Chile, or Charcas (present-day Bolivia)[3] on very long journeys to be ordained. Further, recruiting for clerical life was difficult. The late creation of the Viceroyalty of Río de la Plata (1776) did not put an end to the long periods of vacant bishoprics in the region that in turn resulted in a lack of ordinations.

Later, with the Argentine revolutionary process of the early 1800s, the ecclesiastic situation weakened even more, and the lack of communication between the Church and the Holy See between 1810 and 1858 resulted in the nearly complete absence of bishops and the impossibility of new ordinations.[4] The enlightened romanization and organized parishes of the Catholic Church in the nineteenth century did not reach these societies, particularly in the rural areas, where a large part of the population was scattered until the mid-twentieth century. Only occasionally did missionaries come and offer sacraments to large gatherings. Pastoral activity was not aimed at educating individuals and forming their consciences.[5]

Throughout recent centuries, the only resident ministers were "praying women/men." Only by the end of the nineteenth century did a slow process of revitalization of the Church begin in Argentina with the creation of seminaries and new dioceses, along with the arrival of European religious congregations or the restoration of established religious orders. The more "disciplined" and "parochialized" Catholicism of Italian and Spanish immigrants to Argentina who came at the end of the nineteenth and beginning of the twentieth centuries was not as common, since this region had the lowest migratory percentage with respect to the pre-existing population (according to state data, it was between 4 and 8 percent toward 1914, when the national median percentage was 30 percent).[6] Fluctuations in populations of priests and people continued in this period until the crisis provoked by the Second Vatican Council, which constituted a crisis-and-change type of religious upheaval in Argentina together with the complex political situation and cultural changes of the 70s that shook both Church and society.

Religion from the Mother

Since indigenous people have been isolated for a very long period, they actively maintain pockets of beliefs and traditions related to ecology, health, and religion (they believe there are few walls between the three aspects of life). Both Christian and native traditions exist together, and they make up an important reservoir of customs that challenge urban life with old and still-relevant insights.

Women's faith is fundamental to the construction of the religious experience of the group, because the religious subject is the family or the community in these rural societies.[7] Here faith is *not* the consequence of a decision or a personal conversion: every person is born into it just as they are born into a tradition. Faith is transmitted through the same process of socialization as culture.[8]

Women preserved both indigenous and Christian traditions, and they ensured their transmission generation after generation. It was the mother who passed along a way of being in the world, a symbolic order that makes up a set of relations with God, human beings, and the cosmos. As Luisa Muraro notes, when the mother teaches her children how to speak, she gives them a way of being in the world together with their native language.[9]

The foundation myths of the high-mountain communities are the warp of everyday life. Mothers and grandmothers teach children about their world and history, thus strengthening identity roots. Human life is a multiple framework of stories. Thanks to them, persons, groups, and communities stay alive and meaningful. These narrations are the roots and projections to the future for their members.

Women, possessors of their own symbolic order, help to create a habitat and to contribute to the creation of their small cultural world. The women of these communities have a maternal authority with which they build relationships and construct and transmit family knowledge. Authority is the capacity to create order, understand, and decide about the self. In this sense, praying women of the high mountains wield true authority.

The preservation of tradition depends on authority in these rural communities that are isolated from the processes of urbanization and industrialization. Authority generates continuity by imposing a code of values that guide individual and collective conduct from generation to generation. It is a heritage that defines and maintains order. In this universe, states Danièle Hervieu Léger, religion is the only code that makes sense and that establishes and expresses social continuity.[10] Tradition is thus defined by the authority that is grounded in the past.

The mountainous communities of Tucumán are immersed in a number of representations, images, theoretical and practical knowledge, behaviors, and attitudes that give continuity to the past. Religious collective memory strengthens collective identity because these communities understand themselves as a believing lineage. The rites, the regular repetition of gestures and words fixed in them, facilitate the continuation of their heritage. The production of collective memory shapes the community itself and has a creative and normative character at the same time.[11]

Indigenous Peoples and the Encounter with Catholicism

Most contemporary Latin American scholars examining religious phenomena in their region no longer accept the once-dominant evolutionist perspective that emphasized the linear evolution of history. According to this perspective, secularization would cause reason to prevail over "myth" and the "holy" and an age would arrive in which religion would cease to exist and religious institutions would totally lose their influence. This evolution would take place with modernization and industrialization. From this point of view, many anthropologists have studied the "remains" of traditional religions and carry out inventories of what is disappearing. As the eminent Argentine scholar Fortunato Mallimaci states, however, most recent research analyzes religious phenomena, not only as a legitimizer of a social order, but also as a generator of resistance, struggles, and confrontations.[12] What for some is legalization, for others works as resistance.

In this study, we approach the religious experience of the high mountain communities of Tucumán by attempting to discover signs of native cultural resistance that have survived in their beliefs and rituals for five centuries. In addition, the Iberian baroque aspects of their Catholicism are another bastion for protecting their identity against urban and industrialized culture.

The contemporary religious diversity of the Andean region can be traced to the sixteenth century, when Spanish Catholicism came to America, along with some aspects of African traditions that would interact with native traditions. In this period, three religious worlds with different beliefs, origin, history, symbology, and hierarchies met.[13]

In sixteenth-century Europe, the memory of the "witch hunt" that had tried to control popular beliefs that had escaped church regulation was still very much alive. The persistence of practices and creeds that were outside Church-defined orthodoxy made the autonomy of some of the recalcitrant sectors evident, and it was perceived as an attack against the current state policies. The winning religious culture came to America with a series of intransigencies already institutionalized.

On the South American continent, another history was unfolding. The Diaguitas people inhabited the region I observed. They were conquered and became part of the Inca empire some decades before the Spanish arrived, as the Inca empire (or Tawantinsuyu) extended its influence to the Argentinean Northwest in the fifteenth century. The Inca religious world left its imprint on the Indian-American culture of this region. As recorded in the first reports of the Spaniards, the efforts of the Incas to manage and integrate their territory also included religion as a way to establish ideological unity. However, their efforts could not overcome preexisting beliefs of the tribes absorbed by Inca power.

Christian missionaries arrived in the sixteenth and seventeenth centuries with the memory of war against the Muslims in Spain and with the later experience of the Protestant Reformation crisis in Europe. The Spanish clergy had a solid power structure and ideological control. When the preachers settled in the Viceroyalty of Peru (which included northern Argentina), they refined their conceptual tools to counter any dogmatic deviation. The Inquisition and secular clergy enjoyed a well-defined authority in the cities where most of the population was white or christianized. Away from urbanized places, religious orders were in charge of evangelization and the organizational structure of pastoral care was not as well developed. Hence, the rural world kept their local gods. They survived the extirpation campaigns carried out in the seventeenth century, something similar to the witch hunts of fifteenth-century in Europe. For the sixteenth- to eighteenth-century Spaniards, evangelizing was also hispanizing. Religion was part of the state apparatus and the religious-ideological unification was instrumental to holding the power of monarchy in these lands.[14] However, communal cults persisted in the Inca Empire and under Spanish authority under the formal acceptance of Christianity. Thus, native and Catholic traditions underwent a series of adaptations and mutual influences.

The Calchaqui wars that lasted through the sixteenth century kept the Spanish authorities on constant alert in the southern part of their empire, the Argentinean Northwest.[15] Indian resistance was very strong in this part of the Inca Empire and the Viceroyalty of Peru. Through resistance, communal religious practices were revitalized and messianic movements and pan-regional sanctuaries emerged.[16]

In the context of our study, when the Spaniards arrived, the present-day mountain territory of Tucumán was inhabited by the Diaguitas. This encompassed the Aconquijas, Amaichas, Yocaviles, Quilmes, and part of the Calchaquíes peoples, among others. Lorandi and Bioxadós report that the names of these tribes were related to their place of origin rather than to real groups or identities.[17] The eastern boundaries of the Diaguita area are marked by the frontier of the Tucumán Andes,[18] through which the Diaguitas came to settle in the high valleys such as Tafí and Choromoros in Tucumán.

In this context, Hispanic American Catholicism emerged from the cultural collision between the "baroque Catholicism" of Spain and "Amerindian religiosity" of the native peoples. As Dussel notes, the struggle between Spanish and Indian warriors was also a struggle between the gods of both armies. The defeat of Amerindian forces was for those men the defeat of their gods at the hands of Christian gods.[19]

Christian Parker explains that the origin of religiosity in Latin America lies in the trauma provoked by the arrival of Europeans in these lands. The most sophisticated cults and indigenous religious agents were ousted and repressed, the old gods became "demons," the ancient cults were considered "idolatry" and their priests "wizards." Their devotions became "pagan," their gods were under the light of the new unique God, and they began a slow agony. The natives witnessed their death.[20]

Such destruction was not complete, however. Indians accepted Catholic dogma and liturgy, but their own religious beliefs remained unchanged. The process seemed to be the triumph of the foreigners over the natives, but after some time the transformation was visible in the winning indigenous religion.

Syncretism in the cultural mediations was carried out not only in the dogma or theory but also in the liturgy. Such an amalgam affects the ethos or way of being in the world. Manuel Marzal, a leading anthropologist, defined syncretism as "the formation of a new system originated in two religious systems in contact with one another. It is the product of the dialectic interaction of the elements from the two original systems (beliefs, rites, forms of organization and ethic rules) that causes such elements to persist in the new system, totally disappear, synthesize with those that are similar in the other system or reinterpret themselves for a change in meanings."[21]

Hispanic American Catholicism took what had come from Europe but acquired a local color in these lands. This religiocultural collision would have an influence both in the Indians and in the Spaniards, in the Creoles as well as in the mestizos, thus confirming a state of affairs that would prevail both in the countryside and the towns, although to a lesser extent in the latter. In the rural world, the people remained attached to their old gods, while the clergy—the specialized sector of the new religion—was unable fully to reach the Indian world with their new truths. The removed gods acted as a resistance, causing the indigenous people to become secluded and impervious.[22]

Are They Christian?
Indigenous Religious Experience

Any religious experience implies objects of worship or devotion, mediators and mediations. Religious persons strive to put two realities in touch with one another by means of rituals that "relegate" them, establishing a link between humanity and what transcends it, the "other," the divinity. The following account allows for a deeper insight into what it means to be an indigenous religious person in Latin America. Are they to be counted as Catholic and

Christian? At very least, one might say that they would benefit from another evangelization. But Christians might learn from them such practices as care for the environment, spiritual sensitivity, and remembering the deceased.

THE GODS OF NATURE

The recipients of many of the prayers are Pachamama[23] and Llastay,[24] surviving gods of nature in Indian imagery. Pachamama is the great earth goddess of farming peoples, mother earth, the recipient of many rituals and tributes. Both Pachamama and Llastay have a specific function within the society that harbors them: they are the protectors of soil, fauna, and flora; they control hunting and fishing and, therefore, preserve ecology.

THE SOULS AND THE CULT OF THE DEAD

The belief in the survival of the soul has deep roots in the mountain culture. The soul is not merely spiritual; it is, indeed, the person who can somehow eat and speak. It is seen like a vapor or felt like the wind. The *ánimas* (souls) thus have a certain corporality. *Ánimas* are beings with whom peasants live. All the fear in the mountain is nourished by them. Apparitions, ghosts, screams, the whistling of the *ánimas*, all still force people to practice spells, to show the crossguard of their daggers, to sprinkle the place with holy water, and to make the sign of the cross fervently. Indigenous as well as Catholic tradition with its angels and demons, spirits of the other world, and souls in purgatory make up a voluminous body of legends and myths.

Cristina Ayala[25] tells us of her confidence in the intercession of souls: "The soul I pray to the most is that of Germán Álvarez, he grants me whatever I ask for. If I'm looking for a lost animal, he helps me find it." Irma Ayala[26] also says: "To the little souls I pray before I travel, that I may fare well when I go and when I return. I pray for my children, that they get help in school, that they may have a good memory that they may learn, that they don't steal. The little souls are miraculous and they protect us."

The medieval Christian doctrine of purgatory took hold very strongly in the Andean world of the Argentinean Northwest. We may find numerous prayers that bear witness to the strength of this belief. In an introductory prayer to the rosary used by community *rezadoras* (praying women), we find an intercession for the souls in purgatory: "You know well Mother Mary, that there is no pain more pitiful than the one the poor little souls of purgatory suffer, for them we beg you for their relief, we beg you for their glory."[27]

The rituals about death constitute a central core of Amerindian Catholicism, heir of colonial baroque piety and of the ancestors' cult traditions of the native cosmovision. In the communities observed, the funeral wake for the *angelito*, carried out when the deceased is a child, is one of the best-attended ceremonies. The baby, it is believed, becomes a little angel when it dies, and turns into an important intercessor in heaven. Children have a privileged place in the "holy ground," since all of them are buried at the entrance of the graveyard.

All Souls Day draws a massive assembly of people at the cemetery to pray. This visit is not primarily for a mourning but a gathering to celebrate the place of deceased spirits in the life of the community. Simple wreaths that hang from horse saddles are placed on the crosses of the graveyard, and a large number of candles are lit on the tombs to "illuminate" the souls. The cult of the dead, visiting their graves and praying for them, has a privileged place among the rituals of the high mountain communities.

THE SAINTS AND POPULAR CANONIZATIONS

Indigenous communities do not depend on the Holy See for canonizations; rather, they tend toward canonizing those who had an extraordinary death or an innocent life. These people come to be objects of devotion and are made into local and regional saints. The inhabitants of this region carry out canonizations and generate devotions in the hope that new and sometimes ephemeral saints will listen to their dramatic requests.

The place where somebody was found dead is considered a holy place; a cross is set there and a little monument is built with stones where candles are permanently burning, rogations are chanted, and promises are made because that deceased person is "miraculous." A typical canonization of these communities is that of Mercedes Yampa, a heroic policeman who died frozen in the summit of Raco because great fatigue brought on by his work made him fall asleep and freeze to death. Near the place where he was found, a stone monument was built and a cross was put on it. All those who climb the mountain have to pass by it and it is common to stop, make petitions, and ask for the blessing of the deceased for a safe journey.[28]

The patron saints have the function of a *waka*, or protector god of the local community. The patron saints characteristic of the Hispanic towns replaced the totems of the indigenous clans (animals, plants, or imaginary or celestial divine characters) with which the group identified. The favorite saints, such as St. Mary, are those who protected cattle and other animals or produced abundant harvests, such as St. Isidore the Farmer. St. Martha is considered the patron of household chores, and it is common for women to entrust themselves to her for difficult tasks at home. St. Rita, patron of the impossible, and St. Anthony of Padua, patron of lost objects, are also favorite intercessors. On the home altars, pictures and images of St. Anthony and St. Jude Thaddeus and many more can be found.

Doña Panchita Morales describes the images she keeps in her home altar:

Here we believe in all saints...because, for example, I don't have St. Peter but I pray to him....I don't have St. Paul, but I pray to him, I don't have all the images, but I pray to them....St. Cayetano I have and I ask him that my children don't lack bread, I ask for myself and for everybody...because I see that in some places the poor don't even have a piece of bread....We pray to the almitas, to St. Martha who is the protector of the servants....To St. Rita I pray because she can grant any request, she gets the impossible....St. Anthony is the patron of the lost things.[29]

In the prayer notebook that belongs to Doña Panchita Morales,[30] the following poem is found to invoke all saints:

My sweet Jesus
Look with piety
At my lost soul
For her mortal blame.
My Lord Saint Ignatius, alférez mayor[31]
Wave that flag
For the Lord is going by.
My Lord St. Peter,
God's servant,
Open the door to it
For the love of God.
My Lady St. Ann, sovereign mother
And grandmother of God.
St. Magdalena,
By the cross
Run and stay by Jesus' headboard.
Jesus of Nazareth,
King of the jews,
Do not abandon us
By day or by night.
My sweet Jesus

My life and my love
Save me from sins
My Lord.

Prayers, such as this prayer to St. Michael, are also addressed to angels and archangels, characteristic recipients of colonial baroque devotions:

O glorious St Michael, prince of the angels, guardian of the Church and executioner of the infernal dragon, we wish by your hand and free of blame to present ourselves to the Divine Majesty. Amen.

GROTTOES: CHRIST OF ALTO DE LA POPOSA

Grottoes are scattered throughout the Andean region. In the area studied, the image of the Lord of the Heights of La Poposa is in a grotto at 4000 meters (12,000 feet) above sea level. As one of the villagers from Chaquivil recounts, the reason why such a high place had been chosen was Christ's function as a protector of the travelers from the "spooks" that inhabit the summits and the "mysteries" of the mountain.[32] Another adds that it is a very lonely place, and it was chosen for people who pass by looking for a lost animal to know there is a Christ up there who is looking after the stray.[33]

THE CROSS

The outstanding element among the devotions to Jesus Christ is the cross. There are crosses by the paths, left to memorialize the name of someone who died there, and travelers stop in front of them to light candles and pray. On May 3rd, the day of the Cross is celebrated.[34] Everybody goes to the cemetery or "holy ground" to decorate crosses with flowers and to clean the above-ground tombs. After praying, they share the food and drinks that each one brought. As people from very distant places participate in the ceremonies, a market fair is organized on that occasion for them to sell or exchange their products. The flowery crosses of May become an assertion of life over the experience of death.

A villager, Felix Coluccio, analyzes the different celebrations of the cross of May that are carried out all over the Argentinean Northwest, and the similarity of gestures and rites to those of our feast observed at the Chaquivil cemetery is remarkable. Many times the cross becomes a magic, talismanic element. After killing an animal, for example, and before skinning it, the sign of the cross is made on it with the spilled blood to ask for Pachamama's blessing to get the cattle to breed. When mountain dwellers travel at night they live with "ghosts" that they scare away, "pouring wine in the shape of a cross" or showing their knives to the crosses placed at intersections of paths "to get the spook to go away."[35]

THE HOLIEST TRINITY

The Triune God is named in some ancient petitions that are still recited by the pray-ers. In the prayer book of Paula Velardez, we find the following text:

All faithful Christians are obliged to have devotion with all their hearts. With the holy cross Christ wanted to suppress our pains and died to redeem us from enemy captivity. Hence, you have to make the sign of the cross with your right hand three times, the first on your forehead for God to free us from evil thoughts, the second on your mouth for God to free us from dirty words, the third on your chest for God to free us from evil works, and saying like this: Our Father...Hail Mary Full of grace, Wife of the Holy Spirit, born without original sin, Immaculate Conception. Amen.[36]

VIRGIN MARY

The Virgin Mary, Mother of God, had a fertile ground in the agricultural pre-Christian cult of Pachamama. Many of the Marian cults in Latin America and Argentina arise in places of pre-Christian cults. Evangelists tried to give Christian meaning to the "native holy place." Most Marian sanctuaries emerged in that fashion. Marian grottoes in Chaquivil are holy places along pilgrimage routes. It is common for travelers to stop by to ask for protection for the journey or to light candles in keeping a promise.

THE DEMONS

Baroque Catholicism with its angels and demons found elements in the native tradition that favored strong beliefs. Many gestures of Andean religiosity are directed at neutralizing the effects of the multiple ways in which the "demon" can deceive, curse, or hurt mortals. Mountain dwellers fight against the devil, demons, Satan, evil spirits, and so forth, with their amulets, spells, and magic formulas, among which is the signal of the cross.

The "Salamanca" is the place where the devil lives. Those who have sold him their souls in exchange for wealth and triumph in life go there. Francisca Morales tells us that the Salamanca exists in the mountain: "There's Salamanca in a place called La Isla, near Potrero de las Tablas, we were going to La Rinconada...you can see a black thing, like the entrance to a dark cave or maybe it is just black or there may be a black mineral that gives it this look."

People go to The Salamanca to learn any profession. "If you want to be a good carpenter, you go to the Salamanca and learn...the one who teaches there is the devil, of course, because, who can live there?...They say you learn and pay with your soul."[37]

Maintaining Faith:
Women Ministers and Core Practices

Belief was kept alive through ritual routines conducted by mediators (one of the key roles of a priest of most religions) within the community. The indigenous people acted as if human beings cannot establish relations directly with the Divine. Hence they established bridges or mediators to relate them to the Divine. All mediators, for them, relate to corporality. Humans need to mediate toward the Absolute through ways that are characteristic of their own corporality. Three of the most common practices are processions, home altars, and novenas. Holy water and blessings are also common.

Readers are invited to consider these archaic practices through the light of contemporary papal teaching that regards many ancient religions as containing "seeds of wisdom." Indeed, they may have something to teach us about the body in worship.

PROCESSIONS

The *misachico*, or procession, is among the most frequent modes of intercession for asking for some grace or to give thanks for a favor granted. It consists of transporting an image of the Virgin or some saint on a portable platform. The sacralization of everyday space is carried out by means of these processions traversing paths and ravines. The sacred places to which these pilgrimages go are the goal that is reached after much sacrifice. (Physical suffering or striving is central to this religious devotion.)

The villagers make arrangements for musical instruments, such as a bass drum and violin, to accompany the image in procession to "give music to the image."[38] The procession begins with the image escorted by numerous Argentinean and papal flags with the colors corresponding to each saint or Marian devotion. The flags are waved at the

62

sound of the music. The image has been adorned with flowers and other decorations,[39] and it sways to the rhythm and cadence of those who carry it.

When the procession is over, the image is "untied." Each participant in the celebration approaches and unties a ribbon or a flower with which the platform and the image were decorated while the musicians accompany this gesture with bass drum, *bandoneón* (concertina-like instrument), or violin. Once the rite is concluded, a member of the community, the oldest woman or the person who organized the *misachico* to fulfill a promise, carries out the blessing with the image. This is known as the "treading on," since the image is placed upon the heads of the participants, marking a cross. Thus the image is considered "charged" with grace after the procession, pouring its blessings on the believers.

Secundino Rasgido explains the motives for a *misachico*: "A promise is made to a saint, Jesus, or the Virgin, asking for any need, such as for health if someone is sick, for the animals and for all the needs of the people of the place. Then a promise is made, a candle is lighted for a saint, and the procession is celebrated."[40]

As occurs with pilgrimages generally, the *misachico* produces a community experience that strengthens the pilgrim in social links, in the sense of belonging, and in enhancing communitarian identity. As David Carrasco states, the relationships created among the people who share the rite of pilgrimage make them experience an intense feeling of intimacy and equality.[41]

During a *misachico*, barriers among the members of the community fade; even the angriest feel a common link based on the unifying experience of the pilgrimage. We concur with Virgilio Elizondo that the sense of a pilgrimage "seems to answer a deep necessity of human beings to go beyond the limits of ordinary experience to enter the mysterious dominions of the afterlife."[42] *Misachicos* constitute an "open air liturgy," where contact with nature is an important source of attraction.

Raimon Panikkar argues that "Man and nature belong to each other. They are joined by space...plains, mountains, valleys, gorges, rivers, rocks, trees, animals and men...all are part of a whole and are united by space....Man is also a cosmic being."[43] This cosmic experience is evident in these open air rituals, when *misachicos* are seen traversing the hills and the violin and bass drum, heard from far away, are the signal that attracts many neighbors to join in the procession. Pilgrimage has been a constant phenomenon in all religions throughout history.[44]

HOME ALTARS AND NOVENAS

In the family dwelling, a place is reserved for religious worship. This is a small home altar consisting of a table where the images of the Virgin and saints are placed together with candles with which to "illuminate" them. The family, presided over by the oldest woman or the person in charge of prayer, gathers around this altar to pray the rosary and ask for their daily needs.

Among the most common intercessions are the prayers, rogations, or novenas very often carried out by designated persons who pray (pray-ers). These women were taught by their mothers and grandmothers and are chosen from among the ones who have the gift to recite easily. Generally they use old handwritten notebooks they inherited from previous official pray-ers to brighten up their recitation. Hence, some prayers express ancient contents and manners. In each community, there are one or two official pray-ers and they are always wanted for novenas and rogations. They do not receive any pay for this service, only deferential treatment and room and board.

Novenas are celebrated in honor of different Marian devotions and a number of saints. A novena is arranged in order to ask for something or acknowledge a favor granted or to fulfill a promise. Through the year, many people organize novenas so that in several homes or chapels groups are found faithfully and devoutly praying the rosary at different times.

In the well-worn notebook of Doña Francisca Morales, we find an ancient introductory prayer to the Rosary asking for "victory against the infidel heretics" and "peace and harmony among the Christian princes," expressing a rogation of past centuries:

We offer this part of the Rosary in memory and in reverence to the Holiest Son of God and we beg that our Catholic faith be exalted. Give us peace and concord among the Christian princes, victory against the infidels, and heretics; and the conversion of all those of our trade, of our catholic religion, and true penitence of all sinners. Give the blessed souls in purgatory spiritual and corporal health to all of those alive. Holiest Virgin increase our devotion to the Holiest Rosary and have our hearts feel the wonderful effects of this sacred devotion and give us, Queen of Heaven, protection. Look after us, Our Lady, in all our needs and dangers. Give us the forgiveness of our sins from your Holiest Son and the perseverance in so sacred a devotion so that by serving in this life we may deserve seeing and enjoying eternal glory. Amen.[45]

HOLY WATER AND BLESSINGS

Another fundamental intercession in this religious experience is the use of holy water to bless the most diverse objects. Holy water is considered a very strong medicine in the treatment of disease and protection against any evil. Thus, as priestly presence is very sporadic, many turn to "help water" for the newly born to receive a blessing until they can be properly baptized. According to an old belief, every Good Friday, women gather spring water since on that day everything is blessed by the mystery of redemption. On that day too, medicinal herbs are harvested to be used through the year by those who have the power to cure (many women take on the role of healers) in the conviction that herbs are more powerful if they are blessed.

Conclusion

The long periods of absence of bishop and clergy during the Spanish empire, the decrease of priests during the Wars of Independence, the slow growth of a national clergy in the first decades of the twentieth century, and the crisis of the Second Vatican Council in the 70s brought about the emergence of spontaneous lay ministries in the church of Argentina, especially in rural areas. These lay ministers were mostly women who kept the thread of the memory of the faith in their communities. This faith, imbibed in the baroque Catholicism of the sixteenth to eighteenth centuries, was preserved with the influence of ancestral native traditions.

The richness of this Latin American popular Catholicism has been maintained and transmitted from generation to generation, from grandmothers to daughters and granddaughters, thus making up a feminine genealogy in which the nucleus of religious faith has been preserved and enriched. Praying women of the high mountain communities of Tucumán have learned to save and recount old and new knowledge, like the scribe of the Gospel who learned that the kingdom of God is like the home owner who pulls out from his trunk "new and old things" (Matt 13:52).

Francisca Morales, Berta Gutiérrez, Simeona Pistán, Cristiana Ayala, and Paula Velardez are some of the names that evoke the number of women who, besides creating and recreating life, carry out their every day civilizing, transmitting, and creating a way of being in the world.[46] These women understand their political action by securing life, as Hannah Arendt very well put it, making coexistence possible and space inhabitable, where God also has a place.[47]

NOTES

1. The author is grateful to Lucía Santos Lepera for the data to make this chart based on national censuses and church statistics. This chart should be refined to distinguish the Catholic population from populations of other religions, especially since Pentecostals and other groups brought greater religious diversity to Argentina. See Ana Teresa Martínez, "Religión y diversidad en el NOA: explorando detrás de un Documento Regional de Identidad," *Sociedad y religión* 20, nos. 32/33 (2010): 157–87.

2. The population decreased because the closing of the sugar factory in Tucumán pushed a great stream of migration toward Buenos Aires.

3. For a view on the ecclesial situation in the history of Argentina, see Robero Di Stéfano, and Loris Zanatta, *Historia de la Iglesia Argentina* (Buenos Aires: Mondadori, 2000).

4. Américo Tonda's *La Iglesia argentina, incomunicada con Roma (1810–1858)* (Santa Fe: Editorial Castellví, 1965) offers insights on the small amount of priests in the Independence period.

5. Ana Teresa Martínez, "Religión y diversidad en el NOA."

6. N. Gomez and M. Isorni, "Demografía," *Cien años de historia* (Santiago del Estero: Editorial El Liberal, 1999), 287–308.

7. For a study of the importance of women in the transmission of faith, see Jean Delumeau, ed., *La religion de ma mére. Le rôle des femmes dans la transmission de la foi* (Paris Editions du Cerf, 1992).

8. Juan Martín Velasco, "Religiosidad Popular y Evangelización," *Communio, Revista Católica Internacional* 9 (September–October 1987): 388–400.

9. Luisa Muraro, *El orden simbólico de la madre* (Madrid: Horas y Horas, 1994), 86.

10. Danièle Hervieu Léger, *La religión, hilo de memoria* (Barcelona: Herder, 2005), 141–45.

11. The contribution of Maurice Halbwachs, *La memoria colectiva* (Zaragoza, Spain: Prensas Universitarias de Zaragoza, 2004) is fundamental for approaching the question of the religious memory in the making of a community identity.

12. Fortunato Mallimacci notes the changes in understanding religiosity in "Religion," in *Diccionario de Ciencias Sociales y Políticas*, ed. Torcuato di Tella(Buenos Aires: Emecé, 2008), 304–606.

13. For a synthetic view of this sixteenth-century process, see Luis Milliones in his *Religiosidad Popular en el Mundo Andino* (Buenos Aires: Di Tella, 2008), 607–13.

14. Hans-Jürgen Prien, *La historia del cristianismo en América Latina* (Salamanca: Universidad Pontificia de Salamanca, 1985).

15. The reports on the Calchaquí wars are a fundamental tool to distinguish ethnic groups in the Argentinean Northwest. These documents have been transcribed by Teresa Piossek Prebisch and were published by the National General Archive, 1999. Marta Otonello and Ana María Lorandi, *Introducción a la Arqueología y Etnología. 10.000 años de Historia Argentina* (Buenos Aires: Eudeba, 1987). These studies also add interesting data on the constitution of native communities of this area.

16. Luis Millones, "Religiosidad Popular Andina," in *Diccionario de Ciencias Sociales y Políticas*, ed. Torcuato Di Tella et al. (Buenos Aires: Emecé, 2008), passim.

17. Ana María Lorandi and R. Boixadós,"Etnohistoria de los Valles Calchaquíes en los siglos XVI y XVII," *Runa* 17–18 (1987–88): 266.

18. In the old chronicles, the first men to enter the Calchaqui Mountains are called "Tucumán Andes."

19. Enrique Dussel, *Historia General de la Iglesia en América Latina* (Salamanca: Sígueme, 1983), 1:91. Tzvetan Todorov, *La conquista de América. El problema del otro* (Buenos Aires: Siglo XXI, 2003), also analyzes this confrontation of gods.

20. This process of paganization of the defeated religion is poetically analyzed by María Zambrano, *El hombre y lo divino,* última edición (Mexico City: FCE, 2005), when she speaks about the collision between Roman gods and Christianity. Her insights can be very well applied to any experience of birth and death in different religions.

21. Manuel Marzal, *El Sincretismo Iberoamericano* (Lima: Pontificia Universidad Católica del Perú, 1998), 175–9.

22. María Zambrano, *El hombre y lo divino,* 242.

23. Pachamama comes from the Inca tradition, and she has strong roots in Andean religiosity in general.

24. Llastay is a characteristic deity of the communities studied here. There are parallels with this protective deity of nature, but they are given other names in the Andean cosmovision of the Argentinean Northwest.

25. Interview with Cristina Ayala, Campo Santo de Chaquivil, Tucumán, November 2, 2008.

26. Interview with Irma Ayala, La Ramadita, Tucumán, October 7, 2005.

27. Handwritten prayer notebook of Francisca Morales, La Ramadita, Tucumán.

28. The data on Mercedes Yampa have been collected from the testimony of Agustín Pistán. Interview carried out in Cumbre de Raco, October 30, 2001.

29. Interview with Francisca Morales, La Ramadita, Tucumán, May 2, 2000.

30. Handwritten prayer notebook of Francisca Morales.

31. Colonial rank in pious associations.

32. Interview with Simeona Pistán, Chaquivil, Tucumán, September 24, 2006.

33. Interview with Secundino Rasgido, Chaquivil, Tucumán, May 25, 2008.

34. The Feast of the Holy Cross during May is an ancient celebration that was removed from the liturgical calendar, while the September liturgical remembrance continues.

35. These stories were told by Doña Delfina Chocobar, San José de Chaquivil, March 19, 1988.

36. Handwritten prayer notebook of Francisca Morales.

37. Interview with Francisca Morales.

38. Devotional images of baroque piety have been closely studied by historians of the colonial period. See Patricia Fogelman for diverse styles of such devotion: "El culto mariano y las representaciones de lo femenino. Recorrido historiográfico y nuevas perspectivas de análisis. La Aljaba Segunda Época," *Revista de Estudios de la Mujer* 10 (2006): 175–88, and Patricia Fogelman and Marta Penhos, "Una imagen mariana por los caminos del comercio en el siglo XVII. La Virgen de Luján," *Boletim do CEIB* [Centro de Estudos da Imaginária Brasileira] 11, no. 36 (2007): 1–5.

39. Dressing images, a baroque practice, was unsuccessfully fought by the efforts to introduce a more enlightened piety in this region. See Di Stéfano and Zanatta, *Historia*, 164.

40. Interview with Secundino Rasgido.

41. David Carrasco, "El viaje Sagrado: diversas formas de peregrinación," *Concilium, Revista Internacional de Teología* 266 (August 1996): 623.

42. Virgilio Elizondo, "La peregrinación, un constante ritual de la humanidad," *Concilium, Revista Internacional de Teología* 266 (August 1996): 604.

43. Raimon Panikkar, "Peregrinación al Kailâsa y Mânasasaras," *Concilium: Revista Internacional de Teología* 266 (August 1996): 667.

44. Carrasco, "El viaje Sagrado," 662, remarks that "The itinerant characteristic of human existence is reflected in the Tibetan word used to name a living being, human or not: groba, which means 'the one who marches.'"

45. Prayer notebook of Doña Francisca Morales, San José de Chaquivil.

46. I. Beltrán, Marta Tarres, et al., *De dos en dos, prácticas de creación y recreación de la vida y la convivencia humana* (Madrid: Horas y Horas, 2000).

47. Hannah Arendt, *¿Qué es la política?*, (Barcelona: Paidós 1997), 67.

3

Guatemala: Responding to a Scarcity of Priests

Bruce J. Calder

THE PHENOMENON OF CATHOLICISM without priests in Latin America is richly illustrated by the history of Guatemala. The Catholic Church there has been fighting a nearly constant battle to solve the problem since the early colonial period. The root causes have generally included a large population, an insufficiency of priests, and, for many areas of the country, the maldistribution of the priests who were available.

This essay will seek to answer two basic questions: First, what events and circumstances caused the phenomenon of Catholicism operating with a scarcity of priests in Guatemala? Second and equally important, how have the institutional Church and Guatemalans responded to this situation? The first question is best answered by a brief historical sketch, which will follow below. The answer to the second is more complicated and will constitute the larger part of this essay. To begin, however, the Catholic Church's responses to the scarcity of priests have fallen roughly into two categories: The first was to increase the number of priests, generally by importing priests from outside Guatemala; in more recent

73

decades, there has been a serious effort to promote religious vocations among Guatemalans. The second was to create systems and organizations to increase the involvement of lay persons in the Catholic religious activities, to empower lay persons to manage some Church functions, and, more recently, to proselytize among inactive or non-Catholics. In relation to these responses, it goes without saying that an insufficient number of priests is a problem from the point of view of many Catholics and the Catholic Church. But it is good to remember that there have been and still are groups and individuals for whom the shortage of priests was or is not a problem, but part of the natural order of things or even a situation that offers advantages and opportunities.

Up from the Ashes:
The Political and Religious Context to 1954

While not the focus of this essay, the colonial period is that in which the priest shortage first emerged in Guatemala. While some priests and their religious orders made heroic efforts, the large numbers of Guatemala's indigenous people relative to the comparatively small number of priests meant that the original evangelization was, from the Christian point of view, incomplete, leaving some untouched and many thousands baptized but poorly educated and, thereafter, often neglected. This problem likely increased during the three centuries of Spanish rule, given the tendency of the later colonial Church to locate much of its personnel and institutions in the larger cities and towns, leaving the Indians of the back country to fend for themselves, at least religiously, for much of the time. By the end of the colonial period, the Catholic Church appears to have been a large, wealthy, and influential institution, but not terribly effective in terms of catechesis and evangelization in the more isolated rural regions in which most of the population resided.[1]

The situation of the Guatemalan Catholic Church grew much more difficult after independence in 1821 because of the departure of some of the Spanish-born clergy and, thereafter, the dramatic rise of anticlerical liberalism in the 1820s and 1830s. By 1829, attacks on the Church—which included the seizure of much of the Church's property and wealth, the suppression of male and female religious orders, the elimination of religious education, and the banishment of the archbishop of Guatemala—had severely damaged its capacity as an institution. Although the Church had an opportunity to recuperate somewhat under the conservative dictatorship of Rafael Carrera and his successor (1839–71), the liberal regime of Justo Rufino Barrios instituted even harsher anticlerical measures in the 1870s, which remained in place until the 1950s. The Church was reduced to a shattered shell of the rich and powerful institution that had existed before the liberal attacks. It was small and impoverished, limited by the state to a narrow range of purely religious activities, and was so short of priests that it could not serve even the most basic spiritual needs of many Guatemalans. During the eighty years from the 1870s to 1954, Guatemala, outside of a few urban centers, remained a prime example of Latin America's experience of Catholicism without priests.

Beginning in the 1920s, two things began to change. First, the Vatican under Pope Pius XI began working to end the long conflict between church and state in Latin America and to strengthen the generally weak and ineffective Catholic Church in that region. Second, the political climate in Latin America began to shift, albeit at different rates in different places, with the result that anticlericalism began to subside. The new situation allowed the Vatican to increase contacts between Rome and the Catholic hierarchies of the various nations and to gradually forge diplomatic ties with Latin American governments.[2]

In the case of Guatemala, the ice of anticlericalism began to crack in the 1930s and 1940s. While liberal anticlericalism remained the law of the land until the mid-1950s, the Catholic Church began to experience a slightly warmer political environment in the 1930s and 1940s, perhaps because the Church was so weak and insignificant as to present no political threat, but also because the papal nuncio in neighboring Honduras was courting the vainglorious Guatemalan dictator of the time, Jorge Ubico, as part of a plan to reassert the Vatican's influence in Central America. In 1936 the Guatemalan state agreed to exchange diplomatic intermediaries with Rome. Thereafter, President Ubico, who had his own reasons for wanting the support of the Catholic Church, gradually lifted or ignored some of the most troublesome of the anticlerical laws. He also began to admit a few members of religious orders, both priests and nuns, into the country to provide both religious and social services in parishes, parochial schools, and health facilities.[3] This small number continued to grow after Guatemala's democratic revolution of 1944. While some officials continued to harass the Church with their customary anticlericalism, their liberal attitudes and actions seemed increasingly irrelevant under the two modernizing presidents, Juan José Arévalo and Jacobo Arbenz, of the ten-year revolutionary period (1944–54).

The Plan for Re-Christianizing Guatemala

The 1936 accord opened the way for the building of a more effective Catholic Church.[4] The hierarchy, led by Luis Durou y Sure, the archbishop of Guatemala from 1928 to 1938, worked with the papal nuncio to create a plan for the Church's renewal. The plan reflected the fact that many, if not most, Catholics were abysmally ignorant of Catholic doctrine, that many Catholics had little or no contact with priests, and that many Guatemalans held Mayan indigenous beliefs and followed traditional Mayan practices.[5] In the view of the Vatican and the hierarchy, the situation was so grave as to require a "re-Conquest," the re-Christianization of those who had fallen away from Catholic orthodoxy during years of neglect. To accomplish such a task would require many more priests.

The Guatemalan hierarchy initially advocated solving the shortage of priests with a plan to rebuild Guatemala's hardly functioning national seminary; to do this they would also have to improve the Guatemalan school system, since no uneducated boy could possibly succeed in the seminary.[6] But the Vatican, while it supported the idea of reinvigorating the seminary and helped to procure well-educated foreign priests for the faculty, believed that it would be years before Guatemala could produce many new priests. Thus the Vatican's representatives pushed hard to import missionary priests from elsewhere, using their connections to bring in many or most of the priests and nuns who arrived in Guatemala between the 1930s and the 1950s. Thereafter, the combination of improving the seminary and importing foreign priests and other religious personnel for pastoral work became the basic plan for reviving orthodox Catholicism in Guatemala. In the end, as the Vatican had predicted, the use of foreign personnel produced far better short- and medium-term results than the efforts to revive the seminary.

The relative tolerance of the Church's slight expansion during the 1944–54 period did not create a bond between the state and its largest independent institution, particularly after the 1950 election of President Arbenz, whom Catholic leaders and conservatives in general found too far to the left and regarded as being perhaps even under the influence of communism. While their view may seem to modern eyes an exaggerated, inaccurate analysis of Arbenz's reformist and nationalist programs for social and economic change, its adoption by the Church was hardly surprising. The Vatican, the Guatemalan elite, and the hierarchy were all early supporters of international anticommunism.[7] They associated revolution with the events in neighboring Central American nations and Mexico, where efforts at social and economic reform in the 1930s and 1940s were frequently associated with leftist political actors. Moreover, a significant part of the Church's new clergy had recently arrived from Spain (where most priests were avid supporters of the fascist Spanish dictator, General Francisco Franco) and China (from which the Maryknolls were then fleeing the communist insurgency against the nationalists). The result was a rampant spirit of anticommunism among Catholic leaders and activists in the 1940s and 1950s, a view fervently encouraged by U.S. policy and public opinion.

The Catholic Church eventually became one of the loudest critics of the Arbenz administration and, along with the Guatemalan elite, a major supporter of the U.S.–sponsored coup against his government in 1954. The reward for the Church's involvement was very favorable treatment by the new regime of Colonel Carlos Castillo Armas, particularly the abandonment of all of the old anticlerical legislation in the new constitution of 1956 and increased privileges for the Church in that of 1965. The meaning of the change was that the Catholic Church was free, for the first time in more than eighty years, to begin rebuilding its clerical staff and institutional base. Moreover, it had powerful backers: not only the Guatemalan elite but also the Vatican, the U.S. Catholic bishops, and the government of the United States. All of these players generally agreed that rebuilding the Catholic Church would be one of the best possible ways to prevent the Guatemalans from falling into the clutches of communists or their like in the future.[8]

The establishment of a conservative, pro-Church government in 1954 marked the beginning of a major change in the relationship of the Catholic Church to Guatemalan society. Several important changes occurred. First, the severe shortage of priests and male and female religious, which had kept the Church out of meaningful contact with large numbers of Guatemalans, began to ease much more rapidly than before. Church personnel, particularly foreign missionaries from Western Europe and North America, began to bring formal Catholicism back to large areas that had been badly neglected since the 1870s if not long before. The newcomers, many of them younger and full of energy and spirit, often brought new (or at least different) approaches to such tasks as evangelization and running a parish. But although they were part of a steadily expanding religious presence, especially in rural areas, they were still stretched very thin, frequently serving large expanses of territory with no modern means of transportation and absurdly large numbers of parishioners.

This situation led to a second major change. Priests faced with overwhelming workloads began to search for innovative ways to create activist parishioners who could, with the instruction and supervision of the priest, help carry on the religious life of the parish. These assistants, usually called catechists, were especially useful for serving the villages and hamlets in outlying areas of a parish, which received direct pastoral attention only intermittently.[9] The need for these assistants led to the increased utilization of Catholic Action, a lay movement brought to Guatemala from Europe beginning in the 1930s. This movement, as we shall see below, eventually had a great impact on Catholics and Catholicism in Guatemala.

The Origins of Lay-Based
Catholic Movements in Guatemala

In the 1940s and 1950s, a number of lay-based Catholic organizations were already in existence in Guatemala. They were generally intended to increase the vitality of the Church by involving the laity more actively in their religion. These were usually devotional practices, often imported from Europe, and oriented to urban women of the middle and upper classes. This pattern of prayerful piety, however, did not apply to the two largest and strongest lay groups, the *cofradías* and Catholic Action (Acción Católica). Both institutions represented, at different times, the Church's effort to engage lay persons, to deepen their Catholicism, and to enlist the laity's assistance in maintaining the practice of Catholicism in the absence of sufficient priests. But there the obvious similarities end. The creation of the *cofradías*, lay Catholic brotherhoods formed in the cities, towns, and hamlets of Guatemala, went back to the early colonial period and to medieval Spain itself. In many instances, especially in heavily Indian population centers, they had become one of the primary modes of local religious participation for both men and women and were intimately related to local political and status structures. But the *cofradías* in Indian areas were hardly under the control of priests and the Catholic hierarchy. While they may have originally been created and managed by Catholic priests, as the Church gradually receded from the more remote areas of the countryside, especially during the anticlerical period of the nineteenth and twentieth centuries, the *cofradías* became more and more independent and were increasingly free to adopt a creative mix of Catholic and Mayan beliefs in which priests, the sacraments, and Catholic doctrine played only a minor role.[10]

By the time of the arrival of new groups of missionaries in the mid-twentieth century, the *cofradías* were so deeply entrenched in managing religious affairs, including control of the Church buildings, ceremonial occasions, and the carrying out of most rites, that they became a serious obstacle to the reestablishment of *Roman* Catholicism. There is a body of stories among the missionaries of the 1940s and 1950s about struggles between priests and the *cofradía* members over the keys to the churches, over possession of the churches' furnishings (especially the carved wooden figures known as *santos*), over rituals centered on Mayan gods and demi-gods (such as the folk saint Maximón), and similar matters that led to confrontations so serious in a few cases that the priests had to abandon their parishes and flee for their lives.[11] One lesson of these experiences, at least to many priests and Church leaders, was that lay organizations could not be trusted to function on their own, thus reinforcing an idea that already flourished in the top-down hierarchical Church of the time.

While *cofradías* represented the past, especially in rural areas, and an obstacle to the rural Catholic Church in the twentieth century, Catholic Action constituted the first substantial modern effort to evangelize and mobilize Guatemalan Catholics, rural and urban, on behalf of their faith. Its proponents sought to remedy the weakness of the Church in several sectors of the population in particular, directing it at two groups thought to be far from the influence of the Church and formal Catholicism. The first of these included young urban workers and students. The second focused on the Indian masses of the countryside. To carry out their plan, the organizers of Catholic Action envisioned using the few priests at their disposal to organize small cadres of well-trained lay Catholics (under the strict guidance and control of a priest/mentor). These cadres would in turn proselytize among and train their fellows (urban youth or Indians), imparting the essentials of proper Roman Catholicism. Thus, using only a few priests, they could fairly rapidly increase the numbers of dedicated and orthodox Catholics. In the process, they would give young workers a spiritual formation and an organizational structure that would enable them to resist the enticements of secularism and the materialist philosophies of socialism and communism. In Indian communities, they would use Catholic Action to form groups that would challenge the dominant influence of the *cofradías* and what most priests regarded as a Catholicism so corrupted that its adherents had drifted back into "paganism." With these problems in mind, both of the archbishops of the period, Durou y Sure (1928–38) and Rossell y Arellano (1929–64), supported the use of Catholic Action to form catechists. [12]

The deep roots of Catholic Action were in mid-nineteenth-century Europe, where Catholic activists had organized to revitalize the faith and practice of lay Catholics in the face of liberalism. But Catholic Action in most of Latin America, including Guatemala, was based on a twentieth-century revival of Catholic Action that originated in Belgium, founded by a priest, Joseph Cardijn, in 1924. This new form of Catholicism was gradually labeled as "specialized" Catholic Action, because Cardijn directed the new organization at one group of lay Catholics in particular, young men from the urban working class. Cardijn sought to provide small groups of young workers with both a strong Catholic education and a sense of social and economic justice. These "worker apostles" would then work to convert their fellow workers to a more active and socially conscious Catholicism as a basis for advocacy of workers' rights, particularly for unions and better working conditions. Cardijn's intent was to bring workers back to active participation in Catholicism and to provide a realistic alternative, what Pope Leo XIII (1878–1903) and his successors had envisioned as a third way, a meaningful alternative to the materialism of capitalism and communism.[13] Catholic Action quickly became a major movement in western Europe and in the 1930s spread to Latin America, where its see-judge-act methodology turned out to be very effective. Its existing specialization in young urban workers continued, although new Catholic Action groups formed among younger Catholics, especially secondary and university students, and all branches eventually included women. Equally important, missionaries began to use Catholic Action in rural areas, especially among the agricultural workers who formed the majority of the population in many countries.[14]

CATHOLIC ACTION IN THE GUATEMALAN COUNTRYSIDE

Guatemala was one of the places in Latin America where Catholic Action went beyond its original focus of converting and mobilizing young urban workers. It was initially employed as a tool for re-Christianizing the country's Indian population and only later, after the revolution of 1944 changed the country's political landscape, as a means of reaching young urban workers. Later, as we will see further on in this essay, the see-judge-act methodology was put into use in other important Catholic movements, especially in the Christian Family Movement and the Christian base communities, and even in endeavors associated with the theology of liberation.

Although at first it operated under other names, Catholic Action originated in Guatemala in the mid-1930s due to the efforts of a Guatemalan priest, Rafael Gonzáles Estrada.[15] Catholic Action appeared officially in 1944 when Gonzáles Estrada became an auxiliary bishop in the mainly Mayan diocese of Los Altos, based in the city of Quetzaltenango. Gonzáles established bases for the organization in various towns in his diocese and staffed them with catechists under his direct control who then began to teach Catholic doctrine and to assemble groups of "converts" into mutual support groups in the towns and their surrounding hamlets. The converts, in turn, would work as catechists, seeking to draw others into the new groups supervised by priests. Gradually the program produced favorable results. Its success was further encouraged by the decision of several foreign missionary groups to adopt the catechist system and by Archbishop Rossell y Arellano's endorsement of rural Catholic Action in 1946 as a national organization, the Acción Católica Rural Obrera (ACRO, the name indicating the primary social group, rural workers and their families, that González and Rossell hoped to reach).[16] Over time, ACRO became the leading Catholic lay movement in western Guatemala.

The work of the North American priests associated with the Catholic Foreign Mission Society of America, known as the Maryknolls, produced one of the first great successes of Catholic Action in Guatemala. Maryknoll priests, initially just two of them, arrived in 1943 as part of the Vatican-backed effort to bring more priests to Guatemala (and to Latin America generally). After considering various locations, they chose to work in the Department of Huehuetenango, a large, heavily rural, and mostly Indian area that shares a border with Mexico. To guide their work, they adopted the views and the plan of the Guatemalan hierarchy (and the Vatican), which was to re-Christianize the nation's Indian population. Mayan religious life, focused on the *cofradías* and Mayan rituals performed by Mayan priests, was generally seen by clerical authorities as devoid of the Catholic sacraments and the most basic elements of Christian doctrine (such as the Ten Commandments).

The Maryknoll missionary endeavor immediately confronted a central reality of Guatemalan Catholicism, namely, that areas like Huehuetenango represented a worst-case scenario of Catholicism without priests. Before the Maryknolls' arrival, three priests were solely responsible for trying to serve the needs of roughly 176,000 souls; they departed soon after the two new Maryknolls arrived. In mid-1944 the U.S. missionaries in Huehuetenango numbered only five, and even in 1958, with thirty-six priests, the priest-to-parishioner ratio was still one to more than 6,000.[17] From the beginning it was clear that the priests available could not carry out a proper or successful pastoral program by themselves. The solution lay in organizing groups of catechists to assist them in the work of rebuilding Catholicism.

The Maryknolls' catechetical system began with the notion of catechists *assisting* the priest, acting as lay helpers under strict clerical control. But the enormity of the task of reestablishing Catholic orthodoxy *and* carrying out the normal activities of a parish priest (along with an increasing trust in Indian abilities) gradually led to greater and greater reliance on the supposed assistants. By the 1950s, the catechists, in the words of historian Bonar Hernández, were "spearheading the Maryknolls' program of religious instruction," serving "as 'shock troops' in the campaign to restore Catholic orthodoxy" in Huehuetenango.[18] The great success of the Maryknolls with catechists contributed to their gradual deployment by other missionary and diocesan priests throughout Guatemala, especially in heavily Indian areas.

The use of catechists by the Maryknolls found its inspiration in a variety of sources. One was certainly their knowledge of previous Guatemalan experimentation with Catholic Action through the leading proponent of this approach, Bishop Gonzáles Estrada of the diocese of Los Altos (of which Huehuetenango formed a part). It is also likely that their view of the process of re-Christianizing rural Guatemala was influenced by their contact with Archbishop Rossell, with whom the first Maryknolls spent considerable time when they first arrived in the country in 1943. A third major influence on the Maryknolls was their own experience in China, where they had faced many of the same challenges as in Guatemala, among them the difficulty of communication across cultural and language barriers, a deeply entrenched local religious system, and very few priests. This situation had led the Maryknolls to form groups of religious teachers from Chinese communities through whom they could convey basic Christian doctrine and practice.[19]

These connections prompted the Maryknolls to begin using catechists soon after they settled into Huehuetenango. The first catechists came from cities outside the region (and included both men and women), but because the outsiders spoke Spanish rather than the local Mayan languages, the Maryknolls quickly moved to recruiting catechists from the region they were trying to serve. The system still required translation, however, since the priests, at best, were operating in Spanish (only gradually did some of them learn Mayan languages). This required most of the catechists to be bilingual.

The problems created by language were one reason the Maryknolls moved quickly to create elementary schools in Indian villages (which, along with clinics and local economic development projects, remained at the heart of their program in Guatemala for years into the future.) By the early 1950s, there was a healthy Catholic school system in Huehuetenango taught by Maryknoll nuns and Belgian Sisters of the Holy Family. The new parochial schools provided a serious education as well as a means of creating a body of bilingual villagers, to teach Catholic doctrine more effectively to young Mayans and, in the long run, to create an alternative to *costumbre* (traditional Mayan religious beliefs and practices) and the *cofradías*.[20]

JUVENTUD OBRERA GUATEMALTECA

The second application of Catholic Action in Guatemala was in an entirely different setting, in this case among the secularized Catholic youth of Guatemala City. The Juventud

Obrera Católica (JOC) was founded and directed by a Spanish Catholic priest, Father Gilbert Solórzano, in 1946 and was modeled directly on similar organizations that had emerged from the Catholic Action movement in Europe in the 1930s. Its purpose was to reengage young Catholic workers in their faith and to provide them with a relevant and meaningful set of principles for their personal and working lives based in Catholic social doctrine. This doctrine sought both economic and social justice for workers and a cooperative relationship with employers (who, theoretically, would also adhere to Catholic social ideals and would thus treat workers fairly and pay them well). This utopian vision of the cooperation of labor and capital in a harmonious workplace was closely linked to a religiously and philosophically based anticommunism common to the Catholic Action movement generally. In the words of Bonar Hernández, the historian who has studied Catholic Action in Guatemala most carefully, the "JOC members, or *jocistas*, set themselves to the task of building an army of devout young Catholic worker-apostles that would help the Church 'reconquer' their fellow workers from communism and liberal capitalism."[21]

In its early years, JOC was closely tied to the Catholic Church, its leadership sworn to absolute obedience to the hierarchy. Apart from its enlightened view of workers and their needs it was traditional and hierarchical, controlled (rather than merely advised) by Father Solórzano, aided by a close circle of trusted younger lay associates. This core group became, in effect, lay catechists to a community of young workers, operating both in the workplace and in neighborhoods where the workers lived. Their organizing, including a variety of spiritual, educational and social activities, gradually provided the basis for a vital *jocista* community in Guatemala City and established the JOC as the Church's strongest link to Guatemala's working class.

The major focus of JOC in this period was making Catholicism meaningful to young working people and bringing them back to full participation in the Church and, beyond that, to train them to replicate their conversion experience with other young workers. Thus successive small groups, well-grounded in Catholic doctrine and the Church's social teachings, returned to their neighborhoods to proselytize, organize, teach, and thus to recruit new members to JOC.[22]

JOC's anticommunism was particularly focused on the post-1944 revolutionary government and its labor policy. One aspect of the revolutionaries' effort to improve the prospects of all poorer Guatemalans was its promotion of worker rights and labor unions. While members of the JOC supported workers and their right to unionize, they and other Catholics were concerned that some of the government's leading pro-union labor officials, members of the Guatemalan Labor Party (PGT) and the only group aside from JOC seriously concerned with workers and their conditions, were communists.[23] The Church hierarchy, not to mention most of the Guatemalan elite (which, for reasons of economic self-interest, generally opposed unions of any sort), viewed the labor officials' efforts as a preliminary step in a takeover of Guatemala, its conversion to godless, materialistic communism, the destruction of its capitalist economic system, and a shift to an alliance with the Soviet Union, a fantasy encouraged by U.S. diplomatic officials.[24] JOC, close to the bishops, readily adopted this position. Thus the desire of the *jocistas* and the Church generally to engage with workers faced a contradiction: that, at this point, the Church and JOC would not work with the other Guatemalans most interested in and active on behalf of workers' rights and organizing unions, those on the political left, especially the members of Guatemala's small Communist Party. Rather than forming an alliance, they were engaged in a competition that divided the working class.

After the Counterrevolution of 1954

The overthrow of the revolutionary government in 1954, orchestrated by the Eisenhower administration and the CIA, was enthusiastically supported by the Catholic Church, including the JOC, and the Guatemalan elite. In its place stood a repressive government controlled by or dependent on the military and determined to promote a kind of development that would not threaten the interests of the traditional holders of wealth and power, both Guatemalan and North American. In some ways the new situation seemed ideal for the JOC. It had solid connections to the Church, an institution now greatly favored as a bulwark against the recurrence of the events of 1944–54, and had solid roots in the urban working class. No less important, its main competitors for the attention of workers, active members or supporters of the fallen government, were seriously persecuted after the coup while the JOC was free to continue its activities. But JOC leaders soon found themselves dissatisfied with the new situation: a government controlled by the military and the traditional elite that showed almost no interest in the welfare of ordinary Guatemalans. Moreover, the ruling forces and their rightist allies saw those who held differing views, including unions and others who spoke for workers' rights, as tainted if not controlled by communists, and sought to control them with repression and violence. The leaders of JOC, dedicated to a moderate, middle way between the extremes of unbridled capitalism and communism, used its newspaper, *Avance*, to condemn the continued abuse and exploitation of workers and the use of force in society generally, categorizing these policies as forms of "negative anticommunism" that would actually drive workers and others into the arms of the communists. The way to defeat communism, they argued, was to enact "profound reforms" that would change Guatemala's grossly unfair social and economic structures.[25]

But attempts by JOC and others to bring social, political, and economic change during the later 1950s were fruitless. Military and rightist political groups continued to dominate and Guatemala gradually became a more polarized, repressive, and violent society. By the 1960s, the possibility of bringing reform and social equity began to shrink to the point that the original vision of the JOC, not to mention the social doctrine of the Catholic Church itself, began to fall under suspicion.

JOC's leaders and members, like others, felt limited and frustrated. The result was a gradual process of radicalization, helped along by their own see-judge-act methodology, close contact with other groups working for change, and such outside influences as the Cuban Revolution, the reform rhetoric of the U.S. Alliance for Progress, and the beginning of change in the Catholic Church with the election of Pope John XXIII. Many *jocistas* began to realize that they had more in common with the opposition to the system they had helped bring to power in 1954 than with the system itself. Finally in 1962 some of the established JOC leaders decided to leave the group and to create a Catholic union.[26] In fact, they formed series of very successful unions and union federations. One of them, the Central Nacional de Trabajadores (CNT), founded in 1968, went on to become the largest union confederation in Guatemala. Being in the world of working unions marked the ex-*jocistas* as primary targets of official violence, including assassination, beginning in 1962. By 1968, despite the dangers, the focus of the Catholic worker tradition had shifted almost entirely to working with unions, leaving the JOC with few members and very little visibility or influence. The *jocistas*, trained to think for themselves and empowered by their work, had left the original organization behind.

Catholic Action had a major impact on Guatemala in the second half of the twentieth century, not just on the Catholic Church but on Guatemalan society more generally. While it began as an effort to redevelop orthodox Catholicism in the countryside, the success of its *modus operandi*, using religious revitalization as the basis for a religio-social movement, led to its use with other populations. The first of these other groups was young urban workers, who formed JOC. From there the movement was carried into other urban groups: the Juventud Estudiante Católica (JEC) for Christian secondary students and the Juventud Universitaria Centroamericana (JUCA) for university students. Beyond that, a group of JUCA students were instrumental in forming the Christian Democratic Party in the early 1950s that, in conjunction with rural Catholic Action (ACRO), brought the enfranchisement and political mobilization of Guatemala's Indian population and permanently changed the face of Guatemalan national politics. In addition, the influence of Catholic Action led to the founding of new but related groups in the 1960s. The most important of these was the Christian Family Movement, aimed especially at Guatemala's growing middle class. Finally, the see-judge-act methodology of Catholic Action was brought in to use in new forms of Catholic/Christian activism in the 1970s, when its methodology became one of the hallmarks of the Christian base communities that blossomed along with liberation theology in the 1970s.

The Catholic Church and Lay Movements after 1960

The fifteen years after 1960 were years of great success for the Guatemalan Catholic Church. The period from 1960 to 1975 saw a continued and substantial increase in the Catholic clerical population of Guatemala. At the same time, the established lay movements, urban and rural, associated with Catholic Action continued to prosper. Thanks to the efforts of thousands of catechists, Rural Catholic Action in many towns of the Indian-dominated western highlands had made major gains in the struggle against the power of the *cofradías* and *costumbre.*[27] Even more impressive was the performance of the Christian Democratic Party, born out of Catholic Action's student movements, particularly the university student members of JUCA in the 1950s. Not only was it coming to dominate the newly coalescing political structures of many Indian towns, but its reformist candidate won the Guatemalan presidential elections in 1974.[28]

As Catholic Action continued to prosper, new lay movements began to appear in Guatemala, including the Christian Family Movement, the Cursillo Movement, and, somewhat later, liberation theology and the Charismatic Renewal. Each attempted to get the laity more involved in their Catholic faith, to integrate it more fully into their everyday lives, and to apply it, though in very different ways, to the society in which they lived. The two former groups were organized movements; the two latter were both less structured than was formerly the norm but were very different from each other in their purposes and method. The Charismatic Renewal was based in a more personal emotional and experiential approach, while liberation theology tended toward a more theological, analytical, and political method. These organizations will be explored more fully below.

What happened in Guatemalan society in the 1960s, including religious change, was in part the product of Guatemala's unique circumstances, but also of external forces and events. Some of the most important external influences originated in the international Catholic Church, which during the papacy of John Paul XXIII (1958–63) and its aftermath seemed unusually open and creative. The key events in this period were the Second Vatican Council (1961–65) and, for the Latin American Catholic Church, the meeting of the Conferencia Episcopal Latinoamericana (CELAM) in Medellín, Colombia in 1968. This well-known gathering of Latin American bishops promoted a general spirit of renewal, spurred innovation, and gave a major boost to the spread of liberation theology and its "preferential option for the poor" in Latin America and beyond. In 1979, despite concerted opposition from clerical conservatives, the CELAM meeting in Puebla, Mexico, again endorsed these preferences. Both Vatican II and the CELAM conferences sought to strengthen and mobilize the Catholic laity: to deepen their faith, to make them aware of Catholic social teachings and the need to apply them when interacting with society at large, and to increase their role in the Church. All of this led to a growing tendency to grant more responsibility and even some power to lay persons, women as well as men. This also meant that women religious, another relatively disenfranchised group within the Church, gained in status and authority during this period.

Another accomplishment of this period was the modernization of Church structures, often in the form of new transnational and national Catholic organizations. These facilitated planning and communication across and within national borders and between bishops, members of religious orders, and others. This too was very important to the growth of movements at this time within the Catholic Church. The two most important transnational groups in Latin America were the Conferencia Episcopal Latinamericana (CELAM, the organization of Latin American bishops), and the Conferencia Latinamericana de Religiosos (CLAR), which brought together the various religious orders working in Latin America. In Guatemala, several new structures emerged: one was the national bishops' conference, the

Conferencia Episcopal de Guatemala (CEG), and the other a very dynamic national organization of male and female religious called the Conferencia de Religiosos de Guatemala (CONFREGUA).[29] All these groups promoted communication and education with conferences, workshops, newsletters, and other publications. They also gave a national voice to these different entities within the Church.

The two organizations of religious, CLAR and CONFREGUA, served as sites for the exchange of information, ideas, and innovative practices across the region and within Guatemala itself. In particular, both groups were central to the spread of liberation theology. Such communication was extremely helpful to missionaries serving in Latin America, a large percentage of whom belonged to religious orders or societies. In addition, further communication and planning took place formally and informally within missionary orders, many of which operated in more than one Latin American country. For example, the U.S.–based Maryknolls operated in heavily Indian areas of both Guatemala and Bolivia, providing various opportunities for comparing and learning across national borders. In the case of Guatemala, there was also a good bit of cross-border visiting between the more politically progressive and innovative missionaries, especially with a group of Canadian Xaverian priests in Honduras and with two diocesan priests from Chicago, Leo Mahon and Don Headley, who had created an especially successful project in San Miguelito, Panama. Needless to say, a considerable exchange of information also took place between religious workers within Guatemala.[30]

The Guatemalan Catholic Church was also shaped by the larger political environment in which it operated during the 1950s and 1960s. Within Guatemala, the counterrevolutionary events of 1954 were obviously a watershed moment. Subsequently and more broadly, no event in the 1960s had a greater impact in Guatemala and Latin America generally than the unfolding of the Cuban revolution. Internally it sparked the beginning of a thirty-six-year leftist insurgency in Guatemala, inspired a variety of generally unsuccessful efforts to initiate reforms within existing structures intended to make revolution less necessary, and provided an excuse for an ever-greater level of repression, violence, and military control of Guatemalan affairs. At first the Church continued to benefit. With its anticommunist credentials still intact in the 1960s, the political right still saw it as a bastion against communism, while the moderates regarded it as a source of reforms that would prevent revolution. Similarly, the Church's moderate position appealed to the United States, which had focused its anticommunist gaze much more intensely on Latin America after Fidel Castro and his revolutionaries took power in Cuba. This led to increased aid to Guatemala and, in a U.S. policy innovation, to Catholic-related institutions and projects.[31]

This U.S. diplomatic shift was accompanied by a new policy initiative at the Vatican. In 1961 Pope John XXIII issued a call to North American dioceses to tithe 10 percent of their priests and nuns to Latin America. This move had a major impact on the religious life of Latin America, particularly in countries like Guatemala. By 1966, the various measures to increase Guatemala's clerical population had boosted the total number of priests, nuns, and male religious to 1,432 (including 531 priests), of whom more than 80 percent were foreign.[32]

THE CHRISTIAN FAMILY MOVEMENT

One of the premier lay organizations of the 1960s was the Christian Family Movement, an offshoot of Catholic Action that began in Chicago in the 1940s. In the 1950s and 1960s, the organization spread rapidly through the United States, Europe, and Latin America, mainly as a result of the enthusiastic outreach of its members to others. It was brought to Guatemala in 1961 at the request of Catholic Action leaders working with Monseñor Mario Casariego, then an auxiliary bishop (later archbishop) of Guatemala City in charge of lay apostolates. The Christian Family Movement focused on adult Catholics from the urban middle and upper-middle classes, and was intended to revitalize their Catholicism by providing a meaningful and socially relevant religious experience to these largely new and rapidly expanding social sectors. It gradually spread to other parts of the country, but it remained basically urban and middle class.[33]

The leaders of the Christian Family Movement wanted to move beyond the purely spiritual. It used the see-judge-act methodology of Catholic Action to strengthen the family life of its participants and also to motivate them to understand and to work against the serious social and economic problems that weakened family life in a modern secular society.[34] Thus its members put into practice the Catholic Action ideal of becoming lay apostles. But its purpose does not seem to have been primarily evangelization. Rather, it was focused on using Catholic social doctrine and the Catholic Action methodology to understand and solve the basic social and economic problems, such as poverty, poor working conditions, and racism, that eroded family life. In this sense, the Christian Family Movement seems to have fit well into the social and political environment of the 1950s and 1960s. Given its roots in the anticommunism of Catholic Action, it was an ideal movement to counter the appeal of socialism and communism in Latin America and to support the growing commitment of the Church to enlighten and mobilize the laity on behalf of peaceful social and economic change. The movement also reflected the Catholic Action belief in creating a middle way between capitalism and communism and in the possibility of reform and equitable development within a regulated capitalist system. The latter concept, inspired by fear of the spreading influence of the Cuban revolution of 1959, was also being pushed at that time by such widely publicized projects as the U.S. Alliance for Progress.[35]

The Christian Family movement became a significant Guatemalan lay organization in the 1960s, but its popularity waned in the next decade. Also, despite its moderately progressive tendencies in its early years, the movement eventually acquired a fairly conservative reputation as an organization closely controlled by its priest advisors and the hierarchy and more directed to personal issues within marriage and the family structure than to matters of social justice and reform.[36] Both of these criticisms might be explained by the changing perspectives of activist Catholics after the 1968 bishops' conference in Medellín.

THE CURSILLO MOVEMENT

The Cursillo Movement, formally the *Cursillos de Cristiandad*, was an effort to engage uncommitted lay Catholics more fully in the practice of their faith. Like the Christian Family Movement, it emerged from Catholic Action in the 1940s and remained close to its parent organization into the 1950s. At about the same time, the Cursillo Movement began to spread rapidly from its original center in Spain to the Americas, including Guatemala (in 1962). The movement usually operated at the parish level, putting potential members through intensive three-day courses (*cursillos*); those who continued then attended regular follow-up meetings to renew the Cursillo experience and to fortify the friendships (and thus sources of mutual support) that had formed during the original encounter.[37]

The Cursillo was originally oriented to young Catholic men who were not actively participating in the Church and to practicing Catholics in need of spiritual rejuvenation. The larger goal of the Cursillo Movement was to encourage

Catholics to work together to Christianize the social and political environment, in their families, work places, and communities, to change them and thus "to bring Jesus Christ into the world." While the Cursillos' approach predated Vatican II (1962–65), in the short run the movement was validated and strengthened by the ideas emerging from Rome.[38] A source quoted by Edward Cleary states that by the early 1970s up to 50,000 Guatemalan Catholics had participated in Cursillo course.[39] Some observers believe, however, that in the long run Vatican II actually weakened both the Cursillo Movement and the Christian Family Movement by taking over their issues.

In the Guatemalan context, Cursillo leaders urged their participants (*cursillistas*) to go out into the world and to work together to challenge such things as social and economic injustices, political abuses, racism, and similar matters. Moreover, as lay persons, they were actively recruiting new participants and working to advance their organization as well as to strengthen Catholicism and its impact on society. Thus, much in the manner of Catholic Action, they were mobilizing the laity, evangelizing, and doing pastoral work, even preaching in some settings, all roles traditionally left to priests.

Since 1970: Liberation Theology and the Charismatics

Beginning in the early 1970s, two major lay movements became dominant in the Guatemalan Catholic Church. The first of these was inspired by the theology of liberation, organized around a method of evangelization meant to strengthen the faith of Latin Americans by making religion more meaningful to them by promoting a biblically based consciousness of social and economic realities and thereby the gradual resolution of the continent's most basic problems. This movement was quite dynamic in the 1970s and 1980s but was also amorphous. As a theology, it found expression in many ways, not being a formal structure itself. The second major movement was the Charismatic Movement that emerged, but much less dramatically, beginning in the 1970s. Over the following decades, particularly between 1990 and 2010, the theology of liberation and its projects became less prominent, in part because it had been violently attacked and suppressed by military governments and others. At the same time, the Charismatic Movement, to which many of the more progressive clergy and bishops raised serious obstacles in its early years, became more successful; it was embraced enthusiastically by sizeable numbers of the laity, which led to its acceptance, however reluctantly, by its opponents. Today both of these approaches to Catholicism still exist, although they have changed considerably over the years.[40]

Liberation theology and the Charismatic movement have generally been regarded as polar opposites, which in many respects they were. But they also had some fundamental similarities. In particular, both put a premium on the role of lay persons in the religious experience (though the religious experience was quite different), both put a premium on community, and both regarded conversion, active participation, and continuing evangelization as basic to their movement and necessary to being an engaged Catholic. Thus the two movements represent the most recent responses to the phenomenon of Catholicism without priests, though amidst circumstances much changed from those of earlier periods.

LIBERATION THEOLOGY

Liberation theology, so called because of its central goal, that of liberating society from the sins of exploitation and oppression, grew out of various efforts to work with Latin America's impoverished and marginalized masses. Its practitioners viewed Christianity as a call to create a more just society. Their method involved empowering Latin America's dispossessed masses by consciousness raising, using the Bible as a basis for teaching them to analyze the unjust situations in which they lived and to follow up their new understanding of injustice by acting to change the status quo. Perhaps because of the intensity of Latin America's problems and the frustration of those who had tried to solve them, a sizeable portion of Latin America's younger clergy, many of the missionaries working in the region, some members of the hierarchy, and those lay persons who believed in social justice and change eagerly embraced this new approach and its promise.[41]

Inspired by liberation theology to deepen their commitment to work with ordinary Latin Americans, priests, nuns, and other Catholic activists put themselves into greater contact with the poor, both urban and rural, and with change-oriented organizations such as labor unions, peasant leagues, popular organizations, and political parties with similar social and economic goals. Members of these groups, blocked from access to political power and often suffering repression, frequently became radicalized and sometime supported revolutionary approaches to change. These connections, as well as the very concept of liberation theology, increasingly marked the Catholic Church, its members, and its projects as "subversive" in the eyes of Latin American conservatives and the military.

In Guatemala, the political and economic realities had created a fertile environment for the spread of liberation theology by the time of its emergence in the late 1960s. After the counterrevolution of 1954, Guatemalans had seen continuing political tensions, rising discontent over social and economic inequities, control of politics by an ultraconservative elite, increasing military influence in national affairs, and massive repression in the years 1965–70. Many of these phenomena flowed, directly or indirectly, from the deep divisions left by the counterrevolution of 1954. Discontent with the status quo, especially the marginalization of Guatemala's poor majority, led to serious efforts to bring about a more equitable society. This included a small and ultimately unsuccessful guerrilla struggle and a variety of peaceful initiatives.[42] The latter consisted of political efforts, again unsuccessful in bringing effective change, and of private initiatives, many of which involved urban and rural Catholic lay movements and such missionary-led developmental projects as schools, clinics, and cooperatives. They were successful in providing services to individuals and communities but did not generally change the basic structures that caused poverty and other problems, which led many to believe that something more was needed.

This view was furthered in the early 1970s, which began with an increasing amount of unrest in various sectors of society, including strikes and labor protests, disputes over land, political demonstrations, and growing criminal activity. In addition, a small guerrilla movement appeared in the western highlands. To all of this the military governments of the period responded with increasing repression and violence, including the disappearance and murder of increasing numbers of unarmed civilians considered by the far right and the military to be "subversive." Guatemalan society was in crisis and the situation became more critical in the aftermath of the catastrophic earthquake of February 1976, which most severely impacted the poor and led to a major proliferation of popular organizations, both to aid reconstruction and to represent the needs and views of ordinary Guatemalans, urban and rural. This mobilization, plus the appearance of the guerrilla movement, brought on even stronger repression. One of the main targets of the repression was the Catholic Church, which was associated with efforts at social and economic change and with the increasingly visible theology of liberation.[43]

The situation produced frustration and some disquiet in the religious community. It created a very receptive audience for the theology of liberation and the "preferential option for the poor" among activist Catholics, both the clergy and laity, who created small local groups led by laypersons that were commonly called "Christian base communities" ("*comunidades eclesiales de base*"). These groups were often incorporated into existing structures such as the seminaries, some secondary schools, and organizations made up of priests and nuns, such as CONFREGUA. Some places became known as centers of liberation theology, generally in a few larger cities. In Guatemala City, these included the student center and residence known as Krater, the Jesuits' Centro de Investigación y Acción (CIAS), the residences of the Maryknoll, Sagrado Corazón, and Corazón Inmaculado de María religious orders, and others.[44]

By far the most important and visible impact of liberation theology was the change it caused in the relationships between Catholic pastoral workers and ordinary Guatemalans. Soon the members of various religious orders were living and working with the urban and rural poor. These pastoral workers, along with some diocesan priests, seminarians, and student groups, were founding or assisting Christian base communities and utilizing the consciousness-raising techniques of liberation theology in order to make Guatemalans aware of the unchristian (and sinful) economic and social structures that governed their lives. In areas where Catholic Action and the use of catechists were deeply embedded, such as in the western highlands, the new approach was often joined with the see-judge-act methodology of the older movement. Not uncommonly, the result of these activities was to radicalize some of those participating,

Catholic clergy as well as catechists and other laypersons. Their involvement also led them into greater contact with change-oriented organizations such as labor unions, peasant leagues, popular organizations, political parties, and even armed guerrillas whose basic goals were generally similar. These radicalizing experiences led many dedicated Catholics to sympathize and, in some cases, to join with those who were struggling for change, usually in nonviolent ways but sometimes, especially in the heavily Mayan western highlands, by taking up arms.

Guatemala's government and military responded with a major attack against both the armed and unarmed left, and on all institutions and individuals deemed suspect of favoring significant change. These included unions, social service agencies, cooperatives, universities, and all but the most conservative sectors and traditional activities of the Catholic Church. In addition, the military viewed liberation theology in particular as dangerous, both in itself and by association; any connection was seen as a marker of those who were "subversive." Such an analysis led directly to targeting the poorer communities in which the Church worked, sometimes poor urban areas but particularly hundreds of Mayan villages and, within them, the individuals and institutions associated with the Church such as catechists, the leaders of cooperatives and credit unions, and various others, including those associated with Catholic Action or the Christian base communities. Thousands were murdered, including some priests and nuns. The residents of whole villages fled into the mountains or joined tens of thousands in refugee camps in southern Mexico. Many of the foreign and even Guatemalan priests and nuns, as well as trained lay leaders, were forced to flee, once again leaving the Catholic Church under the control of local communities for an extended period.[45]

The severe attacks by government forces during the 1970s and 1980s, as well as the surveillance, harassment,

103

and occasional murders of activists thereafter, dealt a severe blow to the practitioners and popular structures of liberation theology, mainly the Christian base communities. This repression coincided, moreover, with the Vatican's discouragement of progressive movements within the Catholic Church beginning during the 1980s. The result was a decline in the use of liberation theology within the Guatemalan Church, where it had not been that strong to begin with, and in the pastoral endeavors that utilized the concept. But the concept of liberation theology is still alive in some circles and institutions.[46]

THE CHARISMATIC MOVEMENT

The Catholic Charismatic movement, also called the Catholic Charismatic Renewal, was begun in the United States in the late 1960s and was first established in Guatemala in 1973. It began as a very small endeavor among some middle-class lay Catholics in Guatemala City and very gradually reached other parts of the country and penetrated other social strata. Today, according to recent studies, it is almost certainly the largest lay religious movement in the country. Aside from the fact that the Charismatic Renewal directly affects the lives of many Catholic Guatemalans, it has played a significant role in recent religious developments. Its growing popularity gradually affected the visibility and strength of other lay religious movements, helping to reduce its two main competitors, the Christian Family Movement and the Cursillo Movement, to relative obscurity. It also further eroded the efforts of the proponents of liberation theology, whose base Christian communities and activists in both rural and urban areas were already decimated by the rightist repression.[47]

The Guatemalan Charismatic Renewal began as the effort of several small groups of Catholic lay persons working with a few priests. Its early partisans sought to enrich and renew their Catholicism by adding some new features to their Catholic practices. The first element was a dramatic, emotional conversion experience that would fill the convert with the Spirit of God and a desire to bring this experience to others. This conversion led to joining a Charismatic community. The community offered an environment for ecstatic prayer, lay (and sometimes clerical) preaching, singing and dancing, and the use of some early Christian practices long neglected in the Catholic Church, including healing by the laying on of hands and speaking in tongues. Together these elements created a powerful emotional and religious experience for many of its participants, releasing them, at least for a time, from their everyday problems as well as providing group support and positive energy for returning to the work-a-day world. The Charismatic Renewal also inspired its members to take seriously their apostolic obligation to bring converts into their charismatic communities, often with great success.[48]

In its early years, the Charismatic Movement often faced obstacles, created both by the hierarchy and by many parish priests. Part of the problem was that much of what was new in Catholic Charismatic practice had a strong resemblance to the practices of Pentecostal Protestant congregations, which were expanding very rapidly in Guatemala and Latin America by the mid-1970s. The bishops were also very wary of the Charismatics as a lay movement that was outside their control; the bishops of only two dioceses, Petén and Izabal, encouraged and chose to work with it in its early years. The reason, writes Tim Steigenga, is not hard to identify: the movement's emphasis on "lay local leadership and a personal, non-mediated relationship with God" seemed to threaten "traditional conceptions of Catholic hierarchy and control."[49] Individual priests also frequently shunned or even tried to ban the movement. Some may have done so merely because Charismatic practice was so different from their own.

Other priests clearly opposed it because it seemed to abandon the social and economic concerns that were central to their pastoral views and was so unlike existing Catholic lay movements, particularly those related to Catholic Action and the theology of liberation. Still others believed that the new lay movement divided their parishioners, that the Charismatics had an aloof, holier-than-thou attitude, and that they demanded extra work from the priest, such as special masses for their Charismatic group.[50] Whether or not these charges were generally accurate, the priests' often negative attitude did not stop their growth and in fact drove some Charismatic individuals and groups into the hands of the Pentecostals. Finally, the entire process of Charismatic expansion was likely further encouraged in the 1980s by the harsh persecution of progressive Catholic priests and lay workers during the counterinsurgency of the 1980s that left the Church nearly without established Catholic leaders in many areas of the country.

A variety of factors eventually led to a greater acceptance and success of the Charismatic Renewal in the Catholic Church. One was that early efforts to discourage it failed dramatically; the Charismatic movement continued to grow, often at the expense of established lay movements, especially the Cursillos and groups associated with liberation theology. Large numbers of Guatemalan Catholics, it seemed, preferred the spiritual and emotional boost of Charismatic practice to the comparatively intellectual and analytical work of liberation theology and the Christian base communities. A second factor in the rapid growth of the Charismatic movement was its strong emphasis on evangelization, conversion, and community. The desire for community in some cases led to the formation of covenant communities, groups of Charismatics who lived, prayed, and worked together, pooling their resources and developing new ways to advance Charismatic Catholicism. The innovative efforts of the more dynamic and successful of these covenanted groups led to major advances in Catholic evangelization, to the creation of Catholic radio stations and programs, as well as to numerous retreats, religious rallies, and concerts. Some Charismatic groups sponsored social welfare programs, such as free medical clinics, pharmacies, and the distribution of free clothing and food. These efforts at outreach, combined with the Charismatic style of prayer and worship, seemed to be one of the few effective weapons against continued Pentecostal erosion of Catholicism. Especially when supported by priests and nuns, it seemed to inoculate local populations against Pentecostal inroads. By 1986 these realities led the Guatemalan bishops to issue a cautious endorsement of the movement in the form of a set of guidelines for its official use within the Church, offering it some protection from its critics and leading to further successes.[51]

Another reason for the growth and gradual acceptance of the Charismatic movement was the members' strong and innovative commitment to evangelizing. Similar to their success in forming supportive faith communities within the Church, their efforts to gain new adherents were also more effective than most other groups. This achievement gradually attracted the attention and support of the Latin American Catholic bishops and the Vatican who, deeply concerned about the rapid expansion of Protestant Pentecostalism in their homelands, endorsed evangelization as a central focus of Catholic efforts at the episcopal conferences held at Puebla in 1979, Santo Domingo in 1992, and most recently at Aparecida, Brazil in 2007.[52]

Conclusion

The Catholic Church and the people of Guatemala have been dealing with the relative scarcity of priests for several centuries. The result is a rich history of creative efforts to solve (or to take advantage of) the problem by both the

Church and other actors. While the first of these efforts can be traced back to the colonial period in the form of *cofradías*, the second half of the twentieth century is particularly full of examples of endeavors to overcome the problem. These efforts consisted chiefly of providing more priest and nuns by two means. One was to recruit foreign missionaries to supplement the very small numbers of Guatemalans working in the Church and its institutions. The second was to produce more Guatemalan priests by expanding and improving the Guatemalan seminary system. But the latter involved another much bigger task, that of rebuilding the entire Guatemalan Catholic Church and its institutions, which had been devastatingly weak since the attacks of liberal anticlericals in the 1870s. And a third element of the reconstruction project, which is the focus of this essay, involved the creation of new lay organizations for the purpose of recruiting, educating, and motivating lay persons to become participants in the rebuilding effort. As a result, Catholic laypersons and their organizations have become a significant force in the work of the Church today, including the process of evangelization.

A combination of factors helped to encourage this process of renewal in Guatemala: the Vatican's determination to deal with the general weakness of Latin American Catholic Church in the early twentieth century; the diminishing zeal of Guatemalan anticlericals over time; the rise of new lay movements in the Catholic Church in other countries and their arrival in Guatemala; the rise of anticommunism as a principal motivating factor in Vatican policy, in the foreign policy of the U.S. government, and in Guatemalan politics (leading to the establishment of a pro-Church government in 1954); the concerted European and North American Catholic effort to send missionaries to Latin America in the 1950s and 1960s; and the spirit of renewal that filled the Church in the aftermath of Vatican II and the 1968 conference of Latin American bishops in Medellín.

The result of this rebuilding effort was a much larger, more dynamic, and more effective Catholic Church in Guatemalan. The Church became, for the first time in generations, an effective and relevant voice in Guatemalan society. Subsequently, it has remained so despite a severe attack on the Catholic Church and many of its clergy, institutions, and members in the ten years between 1975 and 1985. The Catholic Church in Guatemala is no longer a poster child for Catholicism without priests. As a larger and more effective institution, it can now produce its own priests and even send some abroad. At the same time, the Church seems to have a better educated and more engaged membership, which contributes in a very positive way to the religious life of Catholic Guatemala and to society generally.

NOTES

1. Two basic sources on the history of the Catholic Church in Guatemala are the several volumes of the *Síntesis del Catolicismo Guatemalteco* by Ricardo Bendaña Perdomo: vol. 1, *La Iglesia en Guatemala, 1524–1951*, and vol. 2, *Ella Es Lo Que Nosotros Somos y Mucho Más, 1951–2001* (Guatemala: Artemis Edinter, 2001); and Mary P. Holleran, *Church and State in Guatemala* (New York: Columbia University Press, 1949). Other works covering more specific periods or topics are noted below.

2. This history is well documented in an excellent dissertation by Bonar Hernández Sandoval, "Re-Christianizing Society: The Institutional and Popular Revival of Catholicism in Guatemala, 1920–1968" (PhD Diss., University of Texas at Austin, 2010). Unlike authors of previous accounts of this period, Hernández gained access to the Vatican archives and to the first-hand reports and other communications of the papal nuncios working in Central America.

3. Hernández, "Re-Christianizing Society," 92–93 and Bruce J. Calder, "Historical Patterns of Foreign Influence in the Guatemalan Catholic Church," typescript (pending publication), 4–5.

4. While this period has been treated in a variety of sources, the following section depends heavily on Hernández for correct details. A useful earlier source is Bruce J. Calder, *Crecimiento y cambio de la Iglesia Católica Guatemalteca, 1944–1966* (Guatemala: Seminario de Integración Social Guatemalteca, 1970).

5. Protestantism, which attracted a very small but increasing number of people, was also seen as an important problem, but a less-threatening one that would become even less significant with the renewal of Guatemalan Catholicism.

6. The sons of the elite, who acquired good educations in private schools, generally did not become diocesan priests; rather they joined religious orders and were trained abroad.

7. Hernández, "Re-Christianizing Society," 93, indicates that even in the 1930s Archbishop Durou y Sure repeatedly denounced communism as one of the three principal evils facing Guatemala, the others being Protestantism and the "paganism" of Guatemala's Indians.

8. Calder, *Crecimiento y Cambio*, 153–63.

9. Priests were normally based in departmental capitals and in larger towns; but the parishes they served generally included many smaller towns, surrounding villages and hamlets, many of which were exceedingly hard to reach.

10. Virtually all scholars, especially anthropologists, who have studied Mayan groups in Guatemala have written about the *cofradías*. Flavio Rojas Lima, *La Cofradía: Reducto Cultural Indigena* (Guatemala: Seminario de Integración Social Guatemalteca, 1988) offers an extensive essay and bibliography on this literature as an introduction to his own study of the *cofradía* in San Pedro Jocopilas.

11. Calder, *Crecimiento y Cambio*, 94–101, reviews some of these cases in the 1950s and 1960s. Anthropologist E.

110

Michael Mendelson focuses on one famous incident in Santiago Atitlán in *Los Escandolos de Maximón* (Guatemala: Seminario de Integración Social Guatemalteca, 1965).

12. Hernández, "Re-Christianizing Society," 115–18 and 206–7 notes the support of Durou y Sure and Rossell y Arellano for catechetics and eventually for Catholic Action itself.

13. The two chief statements of Catholic social teaching at this point were Leo XIII, *Rerum Novarum* (1891) and Pius XI, *Quadragesimo Anno* (1931).

14. Hernández, "Re-Christianizing Society," 243–4. There were earlier versions of Catholic Action in Europe, where it was meant to fight liberalism beginning in the mid-nineteenth century. But by the 1930s, Cardijn's approach to revitalizing Catholics and the Church had been adopted in most of western Europe, though there were small national differences. Generally, it was Cardijn's "specialized" version of Catholic Action that became dominant in Latin America.

15. Hernández, "Re-Christianizing Society," 207; Bendaña, *Síntesis*, 1:120–1.The original names, which suggested groups devoted to doctrine and prayer, were perhaps meant to protect the organization from the repression that liberals might inflict on an organization with the more militant-sounding name of Catholic Action.

16. Hernández, "Re-Christianizing Society," 206–7

17. Ibid., 187

18. Ibid., 205–8.

19. Ibid., 210.

20. Calder, *Crecimiento y Cambio*, 75–83, and Hernández, "Re-Christianizing Society," 198–203. There were government-run schools in some Indian towns and villages, but according to the Maryknolls they were plagued with many basic problems, including poorly trained and often absent teachers, and provided little education.

21. Hernández, "Re-conquering the Urban Working Youth: The Rise and Development of the Young Christian Worker Movement in Guatemala, 1947–1962," (paper presented at the Latin American Studies Association Conference,

Toronto, Canada, October 2010), 1, 9–10. JOC leaders saw liberal capitalism as a root cause of the maltreatment of Guatemalan workers, abuse that led in turn to the advance of communism. Beyond that, they justifiably associated liberalism with the anticlerical persecution and near destruction of the Catholic Church itself during the seventy-five years preceding the 1944 revolution.

22. This summary is based on the excellent exploration of Catholic Action and the JOC in Bonar Hernández's previously cited dissertation and in his 2010 LASA conference paper. Another particularly valuable source on JOC in a slightly later period is Deborah Levenson-Estrada, *Trade Unionists Against Terror: Guatemala City, 1954–1985* (Chapel Hill: University of North Carolina Press, 1994).

23. Ironically, as various authors make clear, the PGT was *not* anti-capitalist, though it did view religion as a false path. Rather, as Levenson-Estrada explains in *Trade Unions*, 18–20, the PGT wanted a "national capitalism" in which workers were treated fairly. The main target of its criticism was the "feudal" landed oligarchy, which the PGT saw as exploitative and a drag on development.

24. For a view of U.S. policy in Guatemala during this period, see Piero Gleijeses, *Shattered Hope: The Guatemalan Revolution and the United States, 1944–1954* (Princeton: Princeton University Press, 1991). See also Richard H. Immerman, *The CIA in Guatemala: The Foreign Policy of Intervention* (Austin: The University of Texas Press, 1982), and Stephen Schlesinger and Stephen Kinzer, *Bitter Fruit: The Story of the American Coup in Guatemala* (Cambridge, MA: Harvard University Press, 1999). Each of these books, especially the work by Gleijeses, documents the role of Guatemalans, including the Catholic Church, in the coup of 1954.

25. Hernández, "Re-Christianizing Society," 299–306.

26. At about the same time, JOC finally got a new and more progressive priest advisor, Father Abel López, who was open to the idea of working directly with unions. It is not clear to me whether he was appointed before or after the

leaders left; the latter would suggest a defensive move by the hierarchy meant to prevent the JOC from falling apart.

27. By 1968 there were three thousand catechists in the heavily Indian Department of El Quiché alone. Jeffery Klaiber, *The Church, Dictatorship and Democracy in Latin America*, (Maryknoll, NY: Orbis, 1998), 225.

28. The candidate, an army officer named Efraín Rios Montt, was denied the office by means of a gross electoral fraud, because ultra-conservatives saw the Christian Democrats as too oriented to reform. Ironically, after having converted to Pentecostal Christianity, Rios Montt took power in 1982 in a coup and proceeded to carry out a bloody military campaign against leftist guerrillas and advocates of change in general (the latter categorized as "subversives," including many non-guerrilla Catholic activists). For the political and religious dimensions of this period, see the excellent work by Virginia Garrard-Burnett, *Terror in the Land of the Holy Spirit: Guatemala under General Efraín Rios Montt, 1982–1983* (New York: Oxford University Press, 2009).

29. The term *religious* here refers to the priests, brothers, and nuns who are members of (and responsible to) religious orders and societies, such as the Franciscans or Maryknolls. This category does not include diocesan priests, who are under the authority of local bishops.

30. The role of these exchanges of information, about liberation theology and other matters, is documented in Calder, "Historical Patterns," 33–37 and 46–47; Phillip Berryman, *The Religious Roots of Rebellion: Christians in Central American Revolutions* (Maryknoll, NY: Orbis Books, 1984), 60; and in James Francis Carney, *Honduras: Un Sacerdote en Lucha* (Mexico, DF: Claves Latinoamericanas, 1985), 74–75.

31. Steven Streeter, personal communication.

32. The total number of priests in Guatemala in 1966 was roughly five times greater than in 1940, with a similar increase in the number of nuns. Calder, *Crecimiento y Cambio*, 59.

33. Augustín Estrada Monroy, *Datos para la historia de la iglesia en Guatemala* (Guatemala: Tipografía Nacional, 1979), 647–50.

34. Calder, *Crecimiento y Cambio*, 127–9, 142.

35. Calder, "Historical Patterns," 19–20.

36. Ibid., 18–20. In the United States the internal workings of the Christian Family Movement led to controversies over the proper role of priests in leading the local chapters. Perhaps because the subject was marriage, lay persons demanded leadership positions and some control.

37. Calder, *Crecimiento y Cambio*, 129–32; Cleary, *Crisis and Change: The Church in Latin America Today* (Maryknoll, NY: Orbis Books), 6–8. In the 1940s, Cursillo participants were expected to join Catholic Action after experiencing the Cursillo courses. By 1949, as an increasing number of participants chose not to do so, the Cursillo movement created its own follow-up groups, the *ultreyas*. Source: French-speaking Cursillo Movement of Canada, "Historical Overview of the Cursillo Movement" (2008) at cursillos.ca.en/histoire .htm.

38. National Cursillo Center, "The Cursillo Movement" (pamphlet, 1995).

39. Edward L. Cleary, "Guatemala: Evangilzation and Mission," in *The Rise of Charismatic Catholicism in Latin America* (University of Florida Press, 2011), 243–344.

40. Phillip Berryman, *The Religious Roots of Rebellion: Christians in Central American Revolutions* (Maryknoll, NY: Orbis Books, 1984), 28ff. This book is the best single work on liberation theology in the social, religious, and political environment of Guatemala and in Central America generally. Also important is Berryman's sequel, covering a later period: *Stubborn Hope: Religion, Politics and Revolution in Central America* (Maryknoll, NY: Orbis, 1994).

41. For an excellent analysis of liberation theology and its practice in Latin America, including Guatemala, see Phillip Berryman, *Liberation Theology: The Essential Facts about the Revolutionary Movement in Latin America and Beyond* (New York: Pantheon Books, 1987).

42. For an outline of the violence of this period, see Rachel May, *Terror in the Countryside: Campesino Responses to Political Violence in Guatemala 1954–1985* (Athens, Ohio: Center for International Studies, 2001), 52–58.

43. On the events and violence of this period, the best source is the three volume study compiled by the Catholic Church's Project for the Recuperación de la Memoria Histórica (REMHI). See *Nunca Más* (Oficina de Derechos Humanos del Arzobispado de Guatemala, 1998). Volume III, *El Entorno Histórico*, is especially useful for understanding the historical context. For an excellent overview of the developments of this period, see Berryman, *Religious Roots*, 173–219.

44. Berryman, *Stubborn Hope*, 10–14. Raquel Saravia and Santiago Otero, *Memoria y Profecía: Historia de la CONFREGUA, 1961–1966* (Guatemala, 1997), 56–69.

45. Berryman, *Stubborn Hope*, 107–44. Saravia and Otero, *Memoria y Profecía*, 89–148.

46. One example of these institutional survivals is the Escuela de Teología y Pastoral Monseñor Gerardi and its training program for Catholic deacons and lay pastoral workers.

47. There are an increasing number of works on the Catholic Charismatic Renewal in Latin America. Some of the best sources are Cleary, *Charismatic Catholicism*; Timothy J. Steigenga and Edward L. Cleary, eds., *Conversion of a Continent: Contemporary Religious Change in Latin America* (New Brunswick, NJ: Rutgers University Press, 2007); and R. Andrew Chesnut, *Competitive Spirits: Latin America's New Religious Economy* (New York: Oxford University Press, 2003).

48. Two basic sources on the Charismatic Renewal in Guatemala are Edward Cleary's chapter on Guatemalan charismatics in *Charismatic Catholicism*, and Timothy J. Steigenga, *The Politics of the Spirit: The Political Implications of Pentecostalized Religion in Costa Rica and Guatemala* (Lexington Books: Lanham, MD, 2010).

49. Steigenga, *Politics of the Spirit*, 22–23.

50. I conducted a series of interviews in Guatemala in 1989 and 1990 and frequently encountered these sorts of complaints from more progressive priests. I also interviewed some priests and nuns who were involved in the movement, which was gaining strength at that point.

51. Cleary, *Charismatic Catholicism*, 241.

52. The Latin American bishops' greater emphasis on evangelization in recent decades is sketched in Edward L. Cleary, *How Latin America Saved the Soul of the Catholic Church* (Mahwah, NJ: Paulist Press 2009), 122–33.

4

Honduras:
Lay Delegates of the Word

Brian J. Pierce, OP

DURING THE YEARS OF SPANISH colonialism, Honduras was always the overlooked little sister of the string of countries that connect Mexico with South America. Mexico City and Lima, Peru were the north and south poles, so to speak, of "New Spain," with Guatemala, Nicaragua, and Panama serving as important stepping stones between the two seats of power. Honduras, with no viable Pacific seaport and very little mineral wealth, was largely left out of the colonial economic scene. There was, of course, a short-lived period of gold and silver mining in Honduras beginning in the 1540s, enough for the town of Gracias to be named a regional *audiencia* of the Spanish Crown in 1544, but it did not produce any lasting effect.[1] Five years later, in 1549, the colonial capital was moved to Antigua, Guatemala, thus putting to an end Honduras's brief appearance in the colonial spotlight. The stigma of being the overlooked country has, in one way or another, remained with Honduras for five centuries, ever since Christopher Columbus, on his fourth transatlantic voyage, made landfall at the bay of Trujillo, where the first Mass was celebrated in August 1502 at a place called Punta Caxinas, known today as Puerto Castilla.

Given that the country had limited commercial importance in comparison with the other colonial centers, there was also less need to establish large Spanish colonies in Honduras. This, of course, caused a ripple effect, for with a reduced population of Spaniards, the presence of Catholic clergy and missionary communities was also kept to a minimum. From the arrival of Catholicism in Honduras to our own times, the Church in Honduras has been poor, with very few native vocations and largely dependent on outside help.

One event during those early colonial years, however, rises above the others like a lighthouse shining into the distant future. The event was the ordination, in 1545, in the regional *audiencia* of Gracias, of Dominican friar Antonio de Valdivieso as the new bishop for the Diocese of León, Nicaragua. One of the ordaining bishops present for the ceremony was his brother Dominican, the bishop of Chiapas, Mexico, Bartolomé de las Casas, the tireless defender of the indigenous peoples of New Spain and an early architect of what later became the Latin American Church's preferential option for the poor.

Las Casas and Valdivieso spent six months together on Honduran soil that year, a time that we might compare to tilling the land for the sowing of the seed—a seed that has taken several centuries to germinate, grow, and produce a ripe harvest. After the ordination, Las Casas returned to Mexico for a while and then dedicated the last years of his life to writing and speaking out on behalf of the indigenous poor of the conquered Americas. Valdivieso, on the other hand, returned to Nicaragua, only to die a martyr's death less than five years later.[2] "Blessed are you who are poor, for yours is the Kingdom of God" (Luke 6:20). It is as if Honduras underwent a kind of prophetic baptism through the brotherly encounter between Las Casas and Valdivieso, opening up the way for a Church that was then and still is a Church both of the poor and for the poor, a Church whose prophetic voice quietly resounds across this once-conquered continent. And that is what brings us to the rest of the story.

Birth of a Lay Movement

We now leap over more than four centuries of history to the year 1966. The Honduran Church is still very poor and still greatly understaffed, with one of the lowest clergy per capita ratios in all of Latin America, second only to Cuba. In other words, it is still very much an insignificant entity on the ecclesiastical "who's who" map of Latin America. Holy Week is approaching in Choluteca, the southernmost prelature of Honduras, bordering on neighboring Nicaragua and El Salvador. Like its neighbors, Honduras has been suffering through decades of political oppression, extreme poverty, and a very high rate of illiteracy. Formal education is rudimentary or nonexistent in large swathes of the country. Religious and catechetical formation is basic and largely devotional, in large part due to the great scarcity of priests and religious, especially in the isolated rural communities.

Not all was bleak in 1966, however, for there was a bit of good news on the horizon as well. A fresh breeze had begun to blow across much of Latin America, a breeze that could be traced to an open window in Vatican City, the very window from which Pope John XXIII, just a few years earlier, had ushered in a new era in the Church by convoking the Second Vatican Council. This fresh breeze had led seventeen Honduran peasants from their rural villages into the town of Choluteca, to attend a workshop that the bishop, a Canadian missionary by the name of Marcel Gerin, PME, had organized, to help prepare people for the celebration of Holy Week.[3] Gerin, himself recently returned from participating in the Vatican Council, was a new face on the Latin American scene, and he knew he had much to learn. Unfortunately, he had not been given much time as an apprentice. Having

119

arrived in Honduras in 1963, he was named bishop of the Prelature of Choluteca just a year later.[4]

So, as Holy Week drew near, it was the peasants themselves who had begged the bishop to send priests to their villages to help them celebrate Holy Week more fully that year. Ever since the founding of Radio Católica a few years earlier, the rural population was becoming more educated in their religion and therefore hungrier for a deeper faith experience. Up until then, about all they knew to do in the almost-permanent absence of priests in their villages was to pray the rosary and, during Lent, the Stations of the Cross. That had been the extent of their communal religious celebrations for as long as they could remember, except for the occasional mass celebrated on a patronal feast day. The workshop to which Bishop Gerin had invited the peasants was his response to their request. The Spirit had moved from deep within the heart of the people themselves, and their bishop, a man attentive to the signs of the times, was responding with true pastoral intuition and creativity.

The three-day workshop for the seventeen lay peasants, or campesinos, ended with the bishop delegating them to return to their respective villages and commemorate the solemn liturgical acts of Holy Week with "Celebrations of the Word" based on the daily scriptural texts. This was, of course, at a time when almost no lay Catholic in that part of the world would have had access to a Bible! Juan Bautista Mejía, one of the original seventeen, shared his memories of the historical event several years later in an interview with Dominican friar Miguel Méndez:[5]

Choluteca was a zone of experimentation for many people. This is where the first agrocredit cooperatives and peasant organizations began...and then in Holy Week of 1966 the Celebration of the Word began....Thanks be to God, I was one of those first seventeen who had the grace of being part of such a marvelous experience.[6]...They gave us a short course and then sent us on our way, with a few materials prepared by Padre Alejandro López, a New Testament, a cross around our necks and a little bit of holy water. The communities received us very warmly.[7]

A few days later, on Palm Sunday, March 27, 1966, the seventeen lay Delegates gathered the people of their respective villages together to remember and celebrate liturgically the solemn entrance of Jesus into Jerusalem. They began by reading a letter from Bishop Gerin:

My very dear sons and daughters: the peace of Christ be with you. As your father and shepherd...I would like very much to be with you personally today and to speak to you....You are familiar with our shortage of priests, and you know that it is impossible for us to visit you this Holy Week, as much as our hearts would desire it....But though you lack a priest, you have a great and steadfast faith, and as you know, even without a priest, everyone has the right and the obligation to praise their God and Creator. It is for this reason that we are sending to you a lay representative...my Delegate. Receive him, therefore, as if I myself were with you. Listen to the words that he will pronounce in the name of the Church....Listen to the Word of God, for through it you will find the...path to life, in accordance with the holy law of God, our Father.[8]

The Delegates proclaimed and reflected on the Scriptures for Palm Sunday, using the New Testament volumes they had recently received as a gift from the bishop. That day something happened in the diocese of Choluteca that changed forever the face of the Catholic Church in Honduras, so much so that, as one Delegate of the Word remembers, "There was such great enthusiasm that at the end of the week the people asked that the celebrations be allowed to continue on Sundays."[9] One can hardly read of this blessed, Spirit-filled birth of a new lay preaching movement in the post–Vatican II Church without recalling the early disciples being sent out by Jesus (Luke 10:1–9):

> After this the Lord appointed seventy others and sent them on ahead of him in pairs to every town and place where he himself intended to go. He said to them, "The harvest is plentiful, but the laborers are few; therefore ask the Lord of the harvest to send out laborers into his harvest. Go on your way. See, I am sending you out like lambs into the midst of wolves. Carry no purse, no bag, no sandals; and greet no one on the road. Whatever house you enter, first say, 'Peace to this house!' And if anyone is there who shares in peace, your peace will rest on that person; but if not, it will return to you. Remain in the same house, eating and drinking whatever they provide, for the laborer deserves to be paid. Do not move about from house to house. Whenever you enter a town and its people welcome you, eat what is set before you; cure the sick who are there, and proclaim to them, 'The kingdom of God is at hand.'"

"Ask the Lord of the harvest to send out laborers into his harvest." That is exactly what the first group of Honduran peasants had done. They asked their bishop to teach them how to read the Bible, how to be evangelizers—bearers of the good news—in a new way. They wanted to give of themselves to their local communities; they only needed a way to do so. It took the vision of a wise shepherd to intuit just how God might be calling this new band of coworkers into the harvest of God's reign. His wisdom is reflected in the letter read by the seventeen Delegates when they gathered the people of their villages for the first Celebration of the Word of God: "Though you lack a priest, you have a great and steadfast faith, and as you know, even without a priest, everyone has the right and the obligation to praise their God and Creator." Yes, a bishop with his eyes and ears open, and perhaps even more than that, his heart open to God's mysterious plan—precisely what Vatican II had called reading "the signs of the times" (*Gaudium et Spes* 4).[10]

Not long before the extraordinary grace of Palm Sunday 1966, the Vatican II documents on the liturgy had envisioned and begun to spell out a wide range of new liturgical possibilities in the event of the shortage or absence of priests. The Constitution on the Liturgy says, for example, that "Bible services should be encouraged, especially on the vigils of the more solemn feasts, on some weekdays in Advent and Lent, and on Sundays and feast days. They are particularly to be commended in places where no priest is available; when this is so, a deacon or some other person authorized by the bishop should preside over the celebration" (*Sancrosanctum Concilium* 35).[11] What happened in southern Honduras in 1966 was the garden of God's word being tended to faithfully by a wise gardener.

In the northern Honduran diocese of San Pedro Sula, a similar bud of new life appeared several months later. In February of 1967, Bishop Jaime Brufau, CM, invited thirty-nine laymen to a course entitled "Initiation Course for Mayordomos." In the Catholic religiosity brought from Spain (Bishop Brufau was himself a Vincentian missionary from Catalonia), the *mayordomos* were lay church leaders often charged with the physical care of the village church as well as with organizing feast day celebrations, processions, and other expressions of popular religion. In some instances, depending on the extent to which they controlled the communal purse and oversaw the expenses surrounding the often very elaborate patronal feast day celebrations, some mayordomos wielded great power in their communities.

What is interesting, however, is that even though Bishop Brufau did not yet know of the experiment going on in the Choluteca diocese, he had also perceived the need to train a group of laypeople to preside over celebrations of the Sacred Scriptures in their local communities. Although Brufau chose to use the old category of mayordomo in the new course being offered, he was not looking for people simply to lead popular devotions and organize processions; rather, what he sought was to infuse the old title with new meaning and a new mission. "New wine," said Jesus, calls for "new wineskins" (Matt 9:16). The new cadre of mayordomos would help the people to discover, many for the first time, the power and richness of the word of God.

This decision to refocus the role of the traditional mayordomo was in no way a repudiation of popular religion and devotion. Anyone familiar with the history of the Catholic Church in Latin America recognizes the extremely important role that popular religion has played over the centuries in nourishing a living Catholic faith in tens of thousands of remote rural villages throughout the continent. As Peruvian Christian Brother Noé Zevallos describes it, "Popular religious practice has survived for centuries in Latin America, and will continue to live on, because in a Church dominated by male clerics, it is one of the principal ways for lay people to live out the priesthood of the baptized. It is and always will be a privileged place of liberating action for lay Christians."[12]

Cristóbal Méndez, a teenager from the northern village of El Ocotillo Occidental, vividly remembers being invited by his local pastor to attend Bishop Brufau's new course for mayordomos:

Another teenager from a nearby village, Candelario Novoa, and I were the two youngest persons attending the course. I was only sixteen years old at the time. To attend the course it didn't matter if you were single or married, nor were there any academic stipulations. In fact, there were people who did not know how to read, and others with only a first grade education. Some of them later learned to read through reading the Bible. At the end of the course, they gave all of us a pamphlet entitled "Celebraciones de la Palabra" that we were to use as outlines for our celebrations and preaching. We were also given a pin that read: Servants of the Word and of the Community. This was to remind us that evangelization encompasses the proclamation of the Good News in its fullest sense: both spiritual and material. And finally, we were told that ongoing reflection materials would be transmitted through Radio Metropolitana, as part of the station's program of popular education by radio. I was asked to be the program monitor for my village, and later was chosen to serve as the overall parish coordinator.[13]

Of course, when we look back today at the beginnings of this new biblical- and lay-preaching movement, which was begun with almost no overall plan or clear-cut goals, we may find it rather unbelievable. One can hardly miss the silent presence of the Spirit at work, guiding the pastoral intuition of two bishops in the same country at the same time, both inspired to place the Bible into the hands of simple, faithful lay peasants, many of whom had received no or very little formal education. The documents of the Second Vatican Council had not even had time to be printed and distributed, but here were two bishops delegating lay people with the responsibility of reflecting on and preaching the word of God in the presence of their local faith community. It was nothing but the beginning of a gospel-centered revolution.

It is commonly recognized that one phenomenon that helped to give strength from the very beginning to the new lay movement of the Celebration of the Word of God in Honduras was Radio Católica's adult literacy program, begun in November 1959 by Monsignor Evelio Domínguez, auxiliary bishop of Tegucigalpa. Using a creative mixture of popular religious devotions, the praying of the rosary, and oral courses in literacy, Bishop Domínguez encouraged a whole generation of mostly rural adults to seize the opportunity and open themselves to the world of reading, writing, and adult catechesis as an important step to overcoming poverty in all its manifestations.[14] It was the first time for many lay people to have any contact with stories from the Bible. And in many cases, as was true for Cristóbal Méndez, many of those formed as community radio *monitores* were also among the first to be tapped and formed in the first courses offered for Delegates of the Word.

Another key element to be mindful of, as one considers the reality of the Honduran Church at this very fertile moment of history, is the groundbreaking meeting of the Second Conference of Latin American Bishops (CELAM) in Medellín, Colombia in 1968 (at which both Bishops Gerin and Brufau were participants). The Medellín conclusions spread like wildfire across the continent, as local churches looked for ways to incarnate the Vatican II documents within the Latin American and Caribbean realities. That very same year saw two important developments in the Honduran Church as well. The first was the decision of the entire Conference of Bishops to adopt as one of its principal pastoral priorities the delegating of persons to lead weekly "Celebrations of the Word of God."[15] The second event was the convocation of the first General Assembly of Delegates of the Word, held October 8–9 in Choluteca, with the participation of approximately six hundred newly appointed Delegates. The theme of the Assembly was "Sunday Worship in Communities without a Priest."[16]

Standing back and looking at these transforming events from the distance of almost half a century, one cannot but be in awe at just how quickly this fire of new ecclesial life and mission spread throughout Latin American. The documents of the Council, with their recovery of the Church's identity as the people of God, and Medellín's call to "evangelize the poor [by] giving preference to the poorest and most needy" (n. 9) helped to ignite hundreds of new pastoral initiatives throughout the continent, the Delegates of the Word being just one of them. Each new initiative spawned others, creating a continental network of workshops and courses among bishops and priests, religious and lay people, as well as building on the work of already existing movements such as Acción Católica and the Young Christian Student and Worker Movements (JEC and JOC). Altogether, it grew into one great fire of renewal—a new Pentecost, fanned by the wind of the Holy Spirit.

Church and Society:
The Movement Takes Root and Grows

Not only did the Church of Latin America and the Caribbean experience a surge of new energy and life in those years, but in some places—and often for the first time—the local Church truly became more and more just that, local: a church whose face was poor, rural, working-class, indigenous, Afro-American, and mestizo, a church that was coming of age, learning to be itself, and no longer just the passive recipient of European religiosity.[17] In Honduras, this represented a very vital step in the renewal of the task of evangelization. Statistics show that in 1973 there were only 211 priests in the entire country, of whom only forty-one were Hondurans. It was a rather bleak situation, even when compared with some other countries in Latin America. "But the laity," notes José María Tojeira, SJ, "were not looking backward and bemoaning the clergy shortage. In fact, the contrary was happening. The lay presence in the Church, especially among the poor, was increasing at a very high rate."[18]

By 1975, nine years after the birth of the Movement of the Celebration of the Word of God, the Honduran bishops were beginning to refer to the new pastoral initiative as an important ministry within the local Church, one that was helping to bridge "the ever-present divorce between religion and daily life, between faith and social commitment, between time and eternity."[19] They moved forward carefully in those early years of the new ministry, committed to ongoing reflection and analysis, while remaining open and responsive to the ever-developing signs of the times. In their Pastoral Message in 1975, mindful of the temptation for some Delegates to adopt some of the clerical attitudes present in certain sectors of the Church, the bishops reminded the Delegates that "what should inspire their ministry in every moment is the conviction that the Delegate is not the owner of the Word which is announced, but its humble servant."[20] What had begun during Holy Week in 1966 continued to mature and change as the years went by.

On their part, the Delegates of the Word helped to usher in a powerful renewal for the Honduran Church in general, an experience of the Word becoming flesh in the here and now of their own particular history and culture. "This new form of preaching the gospel," says Dominican friar Miguel Méndez, "was very motivating for the people in the villages....Little by little the gospel began to echo within their world marked by poverty, lack of land and other social ills. They began to understand the Word of God as something that illuminates the realities of oppression and marginalization by weaving the biblical vision into the world around them. This, in turn, generated a deeper Christian fervor and commitment, spreading to other communities."[21] The fact that the new Delegates had been trained to link the everyday reality of their people with the weekday and Sunday Scripture readings touched and formed the people in a new and profound way. This ancient yet novel approach to biblical evangelization caused a ripple effect throughout the Honduran Church, so much so that even many urban parishes began to ask for Bible courses and for the opportunity to send some of their own lay leaders off to be trained as Delegates of the Word.

Most of the training of the Delegates of the Word over the years has been done in small diocesan-sponsored workshops, aided by the seasonal Celebration of the Word booklets, which contain ideas and reflections to help the Delegates link the scripture texts of a given Sunday with the different liturgical, ecclesial, and social realities of the day. In the early years of the movement, the booklets focused on such themes as "Christians who face injustice," "Christmas: Christ brings us liberation," "Those who work continue the creation of God," and so forth. One of the booklets, entitled "Man and Work," was introduced with a dedication that read: "To our peasant brothers and sisters who suffer as slaves through inhuman work, making us ask just what is God saying to us today. To all the workers, victims of exploitation, and to all who struggle to transform the world into a community of brothers and sisters, we dedicate this booklet."[22] There were also booklets for each of the liturgical seasons of the year. The booklet from the diocese of Choluteca for the Solemnity of Pentecost, 1975, focused on the building of small Christian communities and began with these words:

Historical situations and all authentic human aspi-
rations form an indispensable part of any catechesis.
[For this reason] they should be interpreted…in the
light of the lived experience of the People of Israel,
as well as of the ecclesial community—the place
where the Spirit of the Risen Christ continually
lives and acts. Latin America is living today an historical moment that our catechesis cannot ignore.[23]

As seen above, thanks to the pioneering work of Bishop
Domínguez of Tegucigalpa, the Church realized early on
that in a largely illiterate and rural country like Honduras, it
needed to make use of the growing network of community
and church-based educational radio stations, to ensure that
the Delegates and their local communities, often isolated in
remote mountain villages or thick tropical jungles, would
have access to ongoing formation. The results were phe-
nomenal. New Christian communities began to be formed
and others were strengthened—fed on the Scriptures that
were explained and preached in simple words by lay people
from their very own village.

It is truly marvelous to look back and see how this tiny
seed of pastoral intuition and creativity took root and grew,
nourished in the fertile soil of an open, attentive, and supportive local church. Almost overnight the Bible was passed
orally from the lips of lay preachers to the hearts of simple,
poor Catholic communities across the country. In Latin
America, this was a major step forward in the gigantic task
of evangelization!

The changes happening in the Honduran and Latin
American Church in those years were only a small piece of a
much larger sociopolitical landscape that was undergoing
profound transformation. Throwing off the shackles of centuries of colonialism was not as easy and smooth a process
as some might have expected or hoped. In fact, as the
world's Catholic bishops gathered in Rome for the Second

Vatican Council, Fidel Castro's revolution in Cuba, still jubilant with the overthrow of the Battista dictatorship in 1959, was beginning to serve as a catalyst for social change in many other countries in the region. This, of course, was made even more complicated as the Cold War between the United States and the Soviet Union grew increasingly frigid, dividing most of the world into either revolutionary or counterrevolutionary, Marxist or capitalist, politics and regimes.

In Honduras, a massive and very successful banana workers' strike in 1954 had helped to pump new strength and bargaining power into the peasant and workers' unions, paving the way for the important Agrarian Reform Act of 1962. Unfortunately the very next year, 1963—just three years before the Choluteca diocese's launching of the new lay preaching initiative—a military coup d'état was carried out, throwing the whole country into shock. More than a thousand labor and rural organizers were jailed in the weeks and months following the coup, whose leader, General Oswaldo López Arellano, who was closely linked with the country's landed oligarchy, ushered in one of Honduras's most repressive and dictatorial regimes. The poor, more than anyone else, suffered terribly under the new government's fierce anticommunist policies.

It was into the soil of this difficult yet fertile period of Honduran history that the seeds of the new lay movement of the Delegates of the Word sunk its roots, roots that lost no time in spreading into the rest of Central America and beyond. As one Honduran priest notes, "Even before all the dioceses of Honduras had incorporated the 'Celebration of the Word of God' into their pastoral plan, it had already gone beyond the borders of Honduras. The Choluteca team very quickly helped to organize Celebrations of the Word in the neighboring Republic of Guatemala...and the team in San Pedro Sula set off for the Diocese of Colón, Panama. In

1976 the bishop of Viedma, Argentina initiated a similar experience, assisted through regular correspondence with Bishop Jaime Brufau from San Pedro Sula."[24] And in 1977 the Department of Vocations and Ministry of CELAM held a conference in Tegucigalpa, Honduras on "The Celebration of the Word of God and New Ministries," to reflect on the impact of the new experience of lay preachers in Honduras and the possibilities that this new initiative offered for the rest of the continent.

As the documents of Vatican II and the Medellín Bishops' Conference became more and more available to small faith communities, often in versions using a popular education methodology, so too did the fervor in transforming the social reality from the perspective of the gospel increase. Base Christian communities (CEBs in Spanish) were becoming more and more a reality throughout Latin America, and in Honduras many Delegates of the Word became members and coordinators of these communities. A National Coordinating Council for the Delegates of the Word was formed, allowing the movement to establish common criteria and to form a team of theologians, pastors, and Delegates of the Word in charge of the production of the Celebration of the Word booklets and other materials for ongoing formation. The Honduran Bishops showed their profound gratitude to the Delegates in their Pastoral Letter celebrating the tenth anniversary of the founding of their movement (in 1976):

> With great joy we send this message of friendship and encouragement, as we commemorate the first ten years of the Celebration of the Word of God....We want to express our pastoral satisfaction and gratitude for the authentic evangelization that has been carried out in every part of the country by the Delegates of the Word, who serve with exemplary perseverance and a clear desire to serve God

and their brothers and sisters....From your own communities, leaders have been raised up, trained not only to celebrate the Word, but also with an eye towards the integral development of the communities. In this way, those who preside at the Sunday assembly do not just celebrate the Word, but are "authentic evangelizers." Their role situates them at the heart of the local community, as privileged witnesses to the Risen Christ, called to proclaim His Message.[25]

After CELAM in Medellín (1968), and with the gradual expansion of liberation theology throughout the continent, the Delegates gave greater emphasis to linking the preaching of the word of God with a critical analysis of the sociopolitical, economic, and cultural realities that surrounded them. In 1976, in the tenth anniversary pastoral letter mentioned above, the Honduran bishops reminded the Delegates that "It is the duty of all to struggle for an authentic liberation in its triple dimension: material, human and spiritual" (n. 12). Like many other Delegates, Cristóbal Méndez, the young sixteen-year-old who attended his first course in the diocese of San Pedro Sula in 1967, tried to be faithful to the signs of the times, attentive to what the bishops were saying both in Honduras and in the documents that were being published by CELAM. The pastoral fervor during these years was manifest in an ever-expanding number of peasant and student groups, as well as through the growing network of base Christian communities. Cristóbal speaks of those early years in this way:

> The socioeconomic, political and social reality of Latin America, and particularly of Honduras, urged us to make a preferential option for the poor and marginalized of our country. Because of this new pastoral dynamism, many Delegates of the Word

began to be more and more involved in peasant and political movements, as well as in teachers' unions. Some of the Delegates were even asked to accept leadership positions in these movements, and at first many did so without leaving behind their Church ministry. On my part, I belonged to two very important peasant movements: ANACH (the National Association of Honduran Peasants), founded in 1962…and the UNC (National Union of Honduran Peasants). It was during this time that I also served as a monitor and coordinator of IHER: The Honduran Institute of Education by Radio. There were, of course, some Delegates of the Word who abandoned their ministry in the Church in order to dedicate themselves more fully to politics or to join one of the country's revolutionary movements.[26]

Elected to serve for a period as Secretary of the National Coordinating Team, Cristóbal went on to serve as a Delegate of the Word for twenty-eight years before entering the Order of Preachers, where, as he himself says, "I knew immediately that I was at home—a preacher among preachers." He remembers the challenges in the early years, as each Delegate attempted to translate the documents of Vatican II, Medellín, and Puebla into everyday living:

> I remember saying to myself once when I was preaching, "If after preaching the Word of God for ten years we still do not have electricity, or running water, or a school, then we have preached in vain." And I really believed it! Thanks be to God, the Word fell into fertile ground in the community where I served as a Delegate….Today, in the same community, there are other men and women Delegates of the Word who have organized the community into

smaller Base Christian Communities. There is a women's organization, a music ministry, a cate-chesis program for children and adults, a theater and dance group, and youth ministry....We also have a community development council that reaches out to young people caught in the cycle of drugs, prostitution, youth gangs, and HIV-AIDS.[27]

Baptism by Fire

The early 1970s offered the first real trial by fire of the Honduran Church's aggiornamento. In 1970, after the Honduran bishops published a pastoral letter on social development among the rural communities, the president of the country publicly accused the Church of being an "insti-gator of the unrest in the countryside." The following year, 1971, Father Iván Betancur, a Colombian priest who had recently arrived in the country, awoke one morning to find his parish house, in the Department of Olancho, painted with anti-church graffiti. A few days later dynamite was deto-nated in front of his house, and the town of Catacamas was blanketed with propaganda accusing the priest of being "an imposter, Judas, Cain, a false priest." The tension and con-frontations between the region's wealthy ranchers and poor peasants worsened as each day passed. The Church was being pushed to make an uncompromising option for the poor, and in the rural part of the country, of which Olancho was a part, that meant that the Delegates of the Word, still a largely rural movement, were on the front line.[28]

A year later, in February 1972, several soldiers fired upon a group of campesinos (peasants) who had occupied a plot of idle land in Olancho, with the intention of farm-ing it. Six of the campesinos, who were trying to press the National Agrarian Institute to complete the legal transfer of the land to the peasant group, were killed in the confrontation. The Church reacted immediately in defense of the peasants. The Archdiocese of Tegucigalpa sent a letter to the Diocese of Juticalpa (Olancho), closing with the following expression of solidarity: "May our brother priests and their bishop, Monseñor Nicolás D'Antonio, who at this time have been nailed with Christ to the cross of suffering for the love of our brothers and sisters, know of our unconditional support in these present circumstances." Two months later Bishop D'Antonio and two priests, among them Fr. Batancur, were detained for a short time, accused of "guerrilla practices."

Three years later, the situation in Olancho erupted again. A prayerful march on June 26, 1975 had been planned at the national level to pressure the government to enact the agrarian-reform laws. The National Federation of Farmers and Ranchers opposed the Church's plan, accusing foreign priests of meddling in the country's sociopolitical affairs and of sowing hatred among the campesinos. One group of Catholics from the town of Marcala prayed for the conversion of the president of the Federation, saying that "the mooing of the cows did not allow him to hear the cry of the poor." The nonviolent march continued as planned, with the support of the Church, along with many groups and unions who were pressing the government to adhere more strictly to the promise for reform.

While participating in the march in the small town of Los Horcones, two priests, ten campesinos, and two women students were murdered. Their fourteen bodies were thrown into a well and dynamited. Among them were Fr. Betancur and a North American missionary priest, Fr. Casimiro Zypher. The Olancho massacre became one of the major factors to shape the Honduran Church for years to come. In the aftermath of the massacre, a number of priests, religious, and Delegates of the Word in Olancho, Juticalpa, Progreso, Choluteca, and other parts of the country received death threats and were hassled by authorities. In some other parts, the Celebration of the Word itself was prohibited. The bishops summed up their sentiments a few years later, in a letter to the Delegates of the Word: "The authentic preaching of the gospel often requires a courageous denunciation of all that is opposed to the plan of God....[We should not] be surprised by the persecution. To denigrate and persecute the Delegates of the Word is to denigrate and persecute the Church."[29]

The National Federation of Farmers and Ranchers, in the wake of the Church's growing criticism of the violence and repression, lashed out forcefully against the Church's option for the poor:

> Jesus preached, "Love one another," but our clergy preach, "Hate one another." The lack of Honduran priests has forced the Church to import foreigners for the spreading of the Catholic faith. But this should not justify the meddling of these foreign priests in the social and political issues of our country. The Church should be promoting harmony among Hondurans, not hatred between classes.[30]

Bishop Brufau of San Pedro Sula responded to the Federation with strong words of his own:

> Yes, may all of us put into practice the command to "Love one another," but with actions and not just words. Let us leave behind the hatred and violence, and stop fooling one another. It is not the Church who is preaching hatred. She preaches love, but it is the love of Christ, whose demands have no limits.[31]

As might be expected, the aftermath of the Olancho massacre caused some of the bishops to put on the brakes and pull back somewhat from some of the strong emphasis on the Church's social teaching. The year after the massacre, the bishops tried both to give support for the social teaching of the Church and to sound a note of caution.

> In carrying out the prophetic task of denouncing evils and forming consciences, the Delegate will avoid with great care converting his local pulpit into a political tribunal, or confusing the battle of faith, of which St. Paul speaks, with any kind of partisan struggles....Of course, in the struggle for integral human liberation, the Church does and must get involved in politics, in the sense of promoting the common good. But the Church does not "do politics" in the sense of fighting for the attainment and exercise of power as do the political parties. The Delegate, who presides at prayer in the name of the bishop, cannot assume a role as political leader or party activist, though like any other citizen, he has a right to his own personal political views.[32]

The sudden cautionary reaction caused some tension and confusion among some of the Delegates and other pastoral ministers. The bishops were clearly giving a sign of support for the Church's prophetic mission at a very difficult time, and this must be lauded. But for some of the grassroots ecclesial movements, it signaled a change of course for the Church, which consciously or unconsciously was concerned for its own self-interests and well-being in the midst of the increasing violence.

Many Delegates continued to be engaged in the struggles at both local and national levels, and this, of course, led to the feared yet expected outcome: a number of Delegates and catechists, along with student and union leaders, were "disappeared" and/or murdered during the dictatorships of the 1970s and 1980s. The Sandinista victory in the Nicaraguan revolution in 1979, followed by the deaths of a number of catechists, priests, and religious in neighboring El Salvador, awakened in the grassroots Church in Honduras and throughout Central America a sense of urgency and a commitment to making the reign of God proclaimed by Jesus an historical reality. Many Delegates of the Word and other church workers were faced with the difficult decision between preaching truth and justice in the face of the state's oppressive politics and simply calling for love of neighbor and hoping for the best. More and more polarization arose within the Church itself, not only in Central America but also throughout the continent as a whole.

The martyrdom of Archbishop Oscar Romero in neighboring El Salvador on March 24, 1980 shook the entire Latin American Church, leaving a particularly profound impression on the grassroots Christian communities throughout Central America. Romero's homilies were familiar to many people involved in Christian social action throughout the region. It is no surprise, then, that many lay pastoral workers, including the Delegates of the Word, looked to him for leadership, especially as the situation throughout the region spiraled into ever-increasing violence and civil war. Many people in the rural villages and urban barrios tuned into Romero's Sunday homilies, which were broadcast nationally in El Salvador. For many, especially those committed to a liberating gospel message, Romero was helpful in clarifying the essential Christian vocation of a life of deep holiness and prayer on one hand, and radical discipleship and the option for the poor on the other.

As Romero himself was thrust increasingly into the role of national and regional spokesman and prophet, the understanding of his own call to preach the truth was also sharpened. On November 27, 1977, just eight months after being named archbishop of San Salvador, Romero had this to say about the meeting point between the Scriptures and everyday reality: "We cannot separate the Word of God from the historical reality in which it is announced, because it would no longer be the Word of God. It would be a book of history, a pious book, a Bible that sits in a library."[33] The following year, in a response to criticisms of his preaching, the archbishop laid out the rather simple process that he used each week to prepare his Sunday homily, a process that resembles very closely the methodology used some years later in the preaching courses given to the Delegates of the Word in Honduras:

> First, I study the Word of God that is going to be read on Sunday, and then I look around at my people, and I let God's Word shine on them.... Naturally, the idols and idolatries of the land feel uncomfortable with this Word, and they are very interested to get rid of it, to silence it, to kill it. Happen what may, but God's Word—as St. Paul said—cannot be chained down.[34]

Six months later, Romero referred to the importance of preaching a gospel that takes on real flesh in the concrete realities of history:

> To want to preach without making any reference to the history in which one is preaching, is not to preach the gospel. Many would like a preaching so spiritualistic that it would leave sinners untouched, and would not name those who kneel before money and power "idolaters." A preaching of the gospel that does not reflect upon and denounce the sinful realities that surround it, simply is not the gospel.[35]

One can only imagine the impact that such words would have had on a rural peasant who was learning to preach the gospel each Sunday in his or her local Christian community. Although Romero was officially the archbishop of the neighboring country of El Salvador, many Central American Catholics claimed him as their own. He was not, of course, the only person or priest who encouraged them to link the gospel with the day-to-day situation of their people, but in those years, and even more so after his death, Romero's words carried tremendous weight.

In 1983, almost twenty years after the birth of the Celebration of the Word of God, and only three years after Romero's violent assassination during the celebration of the Eucharist, Pope John Paul II visited Honduras to express his great joy and to encourage the important and innovative lay ministry of the Delegates of the Word. It was, in fact, during these years, from the mid-1980s to the end of the 1990s, that the movement reached the peak of its growth, with as many as thirty thousand Delegates scattered throughout the country during this period.[36] Gathered with hundreds of Delegates of the Word in the northern city of San Pedro Sula, the pope confirmed the fact that this new lay ministry of the Word was indeed a gift for the universal Church:

> It is a true joy for me to be able to pray together and to break the Bread of the Word of God with you who have been entrusted with the mission of preaching the Word and coordinating the celebrations in which that Word is proclaimed. By doing this, I consciously put into practice, in this dear nation of Honduras, the ministry that the Lord confided to Peter [cf. Luke 2:22, 32], namely that of "confirming his brothers," particularly in the preaching of the word of God. It is precisely for this reason that the pope makes his apostolic travels: in order to take to the sons and daughters of the Church everywhere, and to all people of good will, the seed of the Word. Be aware then, as you exercise your ministry in the context of your respective Christian communities, of your cooper-

ation in evangelization with the pope and with the bishops who have delegated you...in your condition as lay persons.[37]

The pope's great respect for the work of evangelization that was being carried out by this courageous group of lay preachers, especially given the extremely volatile sociopolitical situation, is clearly expressed in these words in another part of his talk: "Do not refrain from indicating prudently and wisely the social implications...of the Word that you preach." But even as he encouraged them, he also sounded a note of caution: "And in order to avoid any dangers that might arise, always maintain a close communion with your bishops."[38] The first part was direct and clear: remain committed to the poor and oppressed. The second part, however, concerning "avoiding dangers" and maintaining "a close communion" with the bishop, although clear, again left some of the Delegates with questions. What happens, for example, when the bishop's commitment to the poor and oppressed and the Delegate's own daily experience of violence and injustice are not always "in communion" with each other? Even though John Paul II's words left a few ambiguous gray spots on the ministerial map of the Delegates of the Word, there is no doubt that his 1983 visit was a powerful confirmation of the lay-preaching movement born of the Spirit less than twenty years earlier.

As the violence grew worse, the Honduran Delegates of the Word knew that their vocation had to remain rooted in the paschal mystery of Christ, and that it would not always be easy. They knew that they had been delegated by the bishop to preach the gospel, even when they didn't always know just how to carry out that mission. The caution about avoiding involvement in partisan politics was clear, but the line between the struggle for a more just society and the messy world of politics was not always clear. Again, John

Paul II's words helped to give them courage and strength in their mission:

> Your preaching is very valuable, no doubt. It is the testimony to truth that you give with your lips. But in order for you to be credible witnesses, your life must be coherent with your words. For that reason, your conduct should faithfully reflect what you preach. If that does not happen, you will destroy with one hand that which the other hand has built. This means that your life as a family, as parents, spouses, children, citizens; your fidelity to the duty of solidarity with the poor and oppressed; your example of charity, your honesty, are inescapable demands of your vocation as Delegates of the Word.[39]

Each Delegate of the Word would have to find his or her own way to live carefully and faithfully the difficult relationship between the gospel and the concrete realities of daily life. In 1984, the year after the papal visit, the thirteenth National Assembly of the Celebration of the Word met in Tegucigalpa, accompanied by Bishops Jaime Brufau, Luís Alonso Santos, and Oscar Andrés Rodríguez. Bishop Brufau gave a talk on the relationship between the Delegate of the Word and the various political organizations operating throughout the country. Due to a rising number of accusations and detentions of Delegates accused of illegal political activity and death threats, the Delegates asked that the Church appoint a lawyer who would be available for their legal defense. The meeting ended with the following collective statement, signed by the Delegates:

> We are concerned with the way in which certain groups have spread prejudices, accompanied by a series of unjust accusations, against Delegates of

the Word. Newspapers and radio stations, with insufficient investigation, have then given to repeating these accusations with very little scrutiny....We repudiate the accusations that appeared in Diario Tiempo on October 30, which insinuate that political indoctrination is happening at [diocesan] formation centers in Tegucigalpa and Santa Rosa.[40]

The Delegates knew very well, through their own preaching of the gospel, that Jesus had not sought at all costs to avoid the dangers that his preaching of the kingdom might entail. They also were aware that many committed priests, religious, catechists, and lay ministers had already laid down their lives for the gospel throughout Latin America. For many of the Delegates, then, avoiding dangers was simply not an option. The fact that they had been delegated by their bishop to preach God's word was a matter not to be taken lightly, because they knew that, in the end, it was Christ's word that was being communicated through them. And as Archbishop Romero himself had said, referring to his own vocation as a preacher in the midst of dangers and threats, "My voice will disappear, but my word, which is Christ, will remain in the hearts of those who have chosen to receive it" (December 17, 1978).

At the Heart of the Church

Though the number of Delegates of the Word on the national level has decreased in the last decade, they continue to form the vital ministerial base of the Honduran Catholic Church today.[41] Still a strongly lay and Bible-centered Christian community, a majority of Honduran Catholics continue to be fed spiritually each week through the preaching of a lay Delegate. In 1991 the Honduran

Bishops' Conference celebrated the twenty-fifth anniversary of this remarkable lay ministry in their midst, recognizing the invaluable role of the Delegates of the Word at the heart of the Honduran Church.

> With the vision that this quarter of a century gives us, we can affirm that the Celebration of the Word is a gift from God that remains and continues to bear fruit. For this reason we give thanks to God…[and] we can truly say that the Celebration of the Word of God has been, during all these years, the heart of our Church's ministry.…Know that the Church is proud of you, and like St. Paul, gives thanks to God for you unceasingly, because of the grace of God that has been given to you in Christ Jesus.[42]

One of the very hopeful signs of the last twenty years has been the growth of the number of women Delegates of the Word. Whereas traditionally the men became Delegates and the women served as catechists, today the Church's ministries are more representative of the reality of its members. Women are present in equal numbers today in most of the formation courses for the training of Delegates of the Word.[43] In the 1991 National Directory of the Celebration of the Word of God, we find the following:

> Given the evolution of mentalities, there are many communities today where women are responding to the Lord's call to serve as Delegadas, especially in those places where fewer men are coming forward in response to this call. These women share the same capacity for apostolic work [as the men]. Nevertheless, in order to avoid the common prejudice that religion is only for women and children,

145

we still consider it wise—as a general rule—that Delegates be men.[44]

Having had the privilege of working many years in the mountain villages in northern Honduras, I can attest to the fact that it was always a great joy to see lay women preaching in small rural and urban communities throughout the country. Gloria, a Delegate from a tiny mountain hamlet outside of the northern city of Choloma, often celebrated the word in three different villages on a given Sunday—a spiritual workout that included walking sometimes as much as twelve to fifteen hours in a single day. She is a mother of at least eight children, and often she would have one child on her back and a couple more at her side as she went from village to village, celebrating and preaching God's word. Leticia, another Delegate, has this to say about her call to this ministry of the Word:

> I smoked cigarettes for seventeen years, until one day I said to myself, "Enough of these cigarettes! I want to be a Delegate of the Word." I was invited to the Initiation Course, and...on the last day of the course—Sunday morning—we were taken to the chapel at 6am. I heard a voice within me saying, "What have you come for? Who brought you here? Why are you here?" Suddenly I felt the call within me much stronger. I was filled with the love and mercy of God, and to this day it fills me to share my faith with the brothers and sisters of my community, who daily face so many problems....From the very first day that I stood in the pulpit to preach until today, I have always experienced the same thing: it is not I who speak, but God who gives me words so that others can feel strengthened by God's Word.[45]

Of course, there continues to be the occasional impassioned speech at diocesan or national gatherings of Delegates of the Word as to why women should not be accepted into this ministry, but the Honduran Church has wisely let itself be led by the Holy Spirit on this point. And anyway, at this juncture, the renewal of the faith of the Honduran people is moving forward, not backward, and thanks to the wisdom of the post-Council years, an important path has been opened for all times.

There are many ongoing challenges in Honduras today. Just recently, the country was again thrown into political turmoil following the political coup d'état that sparked a new wave of violence in the months leading up to the 2009 presidential elections. Unfortunately, this is not something unique to Honduras. Most of Latin America continues to struggle daily to survive, frequently left to eat the scraps that fall from the table of neoliberal economics and the ever-changing global shifts of power. Honduras, plagued by a curse that dates back to colonial times, fluctuates annually between second and third place in the race for "poorest nation" status in Latin America, vying for the spot along with Nicaragua and Bolivia. Haiti, of course, always wins first place, with its closest competitor lagging far behind.

The daily challenges for the Delegates of the Word in Honduras are constant. Many delegates are confronted with the very practical reality of choosing between attending a Scripture course at the diocesan formation center or a week of work in the cornfields or a garment (*maquila*) factory, in order to put the daily bread on the family table. Some have had to migrate to the cities or, in an ever-growing number of cases, to the United States, thus losing touch with their villages, and in some cases, with their faith. And a few have found a new home in one of the many evangelical churches, where they can earn some money by preaching—something that wisely has been kept out of the Delegates of the Word movement. The challenges are unending.

Several years ago, as our Dominican team was ending a preaching course for Delegates, one of the participants asked to speak to the group. He shared with all of us the sacrifices that he had made in order to be able to attend the course, knowing that he would return home after four days away with neither money nor food for his family. When he finished speaking, he added, with the profound humility that often marks the lives of the poor, "If anyone can spare just a little bit of food or money, I would be most grateful. I would like to return home with something to eat for my children." It was just one of the many times during our formation courses with the Delegates that we were aware that, though we were teaching the Delegates scripture and preaching, it was they who were teaching us what it means to really live, each day, the transforming power of the word of God.

I would like to close with the story of one Delegate of the Word—a peasant man by the name of Felipe Huete. On May 3, 1991, Felipe Huete, along with several other campesino family members and companions, was gunned down on the land that the group owned and worked as a cooperative in the small coastal village of El Astillero. An Army colonel had decided that he wanted the land, and he had sent a group of soldiers one night to clear the peasant families off and claim it for himself. When the campesinos heard the soldiers approaching in the darkness, they walked toward them, with Felipe at the head. The survivors later recounted that Don Felipe stepped forward and spoke to the soldiers, "Let us dialogue." The response was a barrage of bullets, leaving several members of the cooperative dead or wounded. Not long before the fatal incident, Don Felipe had been seen sitting with his Bible in hand, scribbling down a few notes for his upcoming Sunday preaching. The scrap of paper that he had jotted his notes down on was later found. On it were written the following words, summarizing the central theme of his upcoming preaching: "The earth is a gift of God, and one to be shared in love." He gave his life for the very gospel that he was preparing to preach, the gospel he believed in so fully.

Father Elías Ruiz, pastor of the local parish and friend of the families from the cooperative, was notified and arrived a few hours after the massacre, just as the bodies had been laid out in the home of Don Felipe. He describes the scene:

> I saw Doña Dominga [Felipe's wife], washing the face of her husband, immersed in a sea of suffering, but strong…doing what she knew she had to do. At that moment the image of the Virgin Mary came to me, standing at the foot of the Cross.…Next to the body of Don Felipe, was the body of her son, Ciriaco, being washed by his wife, Bertilia, and next to it, the body of her son-in-law, Salomón, caressed by the tears of his young wife, Isidora. And next to the wall was the body of her nephew, Mártir Huete, in the arms of his wife, Trinidad.…I think I went to each of the women and embraced them, unable to utter a single word. And then I found myself standing again—speechless—in front of Don Felipe. [I could almost see] his hand lifted up, asking for dialogue, as the bullets rained down. Even though the bodies were lifeless, there were rivers of life pulsating from the bodies of the four women, struggling to give room for their tears, their breasts heaving with pain. I said a prayer…and then walked out to give my indignation some space to breathe. I turned to some of the journalists that had arrived and asked them to cry out [to the world] about this tragic reality.[46]

The year following the massacre, our Dominican preaching team was privileged to have one of Felipe Huete's sons,

Reinaldo, in a preaching course for Delegates of the Word, held in the very parish where his father had served for many years as a Delegate. At the beginning session, we asked the Delegates to share with the group how they had been called to this particular ministry. We were not aware at first that Reinaldo was the son of Don Felipe, until he shared his story. He told us that his father, just a week before being killed, had turned to him one day and handed him his Bible, telling him that if anything ever happened to him, he wanted Reinaldo to take over the ministry of preaching for the community. Reinaldo said to those of us gathered that day:

> I tried to refuse, but my father insisted. Why, I thought, is he giving me his Bible? He needs it for his Sunday preaching! Of course, we certainly never expected him to be gone a week later. The Sunday after my father's death, we gathered in the Church—as we always did—for the Celebration of the Word. No one got up to preach. I had my father's Bible with me, and it was burning in my hands, but I couldn't move. When the following Sunday came around, I knew I had to stand up. I had never spoken before a group of people, but something gave me the strength to stand up and speak some words that day. I did it for my father. And that is the story that brings me here today, and why I feel I am being called to be a Delegate of the Word.[47]

Jesus had proclaimed, "Unless the grain of wheat falls to the ground and dies, it remains just a single grain, but if it dies, it bears much fruit" (John 12:24). The Honduran Church, thanks to the grace of God, has been harvesting the fruit of God's word through the preaching of lay Delegates for almost half a century. It is a word that has been watered on many occasions by the blood of contemporary martyrs.

Tens of thousands of people have been evangelized during these years, thanks to this tiny seed of the gospel, sown and cared for at the right moment and by the right people. It is an example of one of those *kairos* moments that God graciously permits, and in this case, one that was met by the faithful response of many people.

I am personally grateful to have been a witness and a participant in this gospel-centered lay movement for a significant part of my life as a Dominican friar. It continues to fill me with hope today, and is a reminder that, for all of us who call the Church our home, we must not forget that we are always capable of growing and changing and being open to the surprises of the Holy Spirit and the ever-new and -renewing word of God. It is an invitation that, like the seed of the gospel itself, requires a dying that bears new life. But the promise is life and freedom, the gratuitous gift of the reign of God. As Jesus himself said, "If you make my Word your home, you will be my disciples. You will know the truth, and the truth will set you free" (John 8:31–32).

NOTES

1. The regional *audiencia* was a Spanish governmental unit composed of both judicial and legislative functions, whose president held the additional titles of governor and captain general.

2. Having just arrived from Spain, Antonio de Valdivieso made his way to the town of Gracias, Honduras for the ordination, scheduled for May of 1545. Little did the newly named prelate know, but his ordination was to be delayed for six months, due to the difficulty in bringing together the three ordaining bishops called for by canon law. Bishop Marroquín of Guatemala and Bishop Pedraza of Honduras were both delayed in arriving, leaving Valdivieso alone with the one bishop who had arrived on time: the new bishop of Chiapas, Mexico, Bartolomé de las Casas. As one author points out, "The forced stay of both [bish-

ops]...during several months offered, without a doubt, an important time to share experiences and to encourage each other in the face of difficulties." Valdivieso was finally ordained on November 8, 1545. Unfortunately, his martyrdom in Nicaragua in February 1550, less than five years later—the result of his own courageous work on behalf of the indigenous population—stands almost as an omen for the entire Church of Central America, a Church washed in the blood of the martyrs. José Alvarez Lobo, *Fray Antonio de Valdivieso, OP: Obispo Mártir de Nicaragua 1544–1550* (Managua: Editorial Lascasiana, 1992), 24.

3. The archbishop of Tegucigalpa, Honduras, Monseñor José de la Cruz Turcios y Barahona, was responsible for initiating a new wave of foreign missionary activity in Honduras in the mid-1950s. One of the first groups to respond was the PME, or Xaverian Missionary Fathers, from Canada, who arrived in 1955. Bishop Gerin was a member of this Canadian missionary society. Cited from an unpublished master's thesis by Fray Miguel Méndez, OP: "Los Delegados de la Palabra de Dios en el Departamento de Cortés, Diócesis de San Pedro Sula, Honduras: Estudio Teológico-Pastoral" (National University of Costa Rica, School of Humanities, Heredia, Costa Rica, November 2003), 24. Here onward: Miguel Méndez, OP, "Los Delegados de la Palabra de Dios."

4. "It is clear that the situation of the Honduran Church was in need of urgent changes, including new pastoral methods and an updated ecclesiastical structure. Beginning in the decade of the 50's there had been efforts made to respond to the situation in an organized way, but in 1965 the Honduran Church was still trying to organize itself in prelatures, vicariates and new dioceses. The diocesan clergy were in much need of updating, but the resources and personnel were so limited that such a task was almost overwhelming." Cited in Miguel Méndez, OP, "Los Delegados de la Palabra de Dios," 26.

5. I owe an enormous amount of thanks to my Dominican brother, Miguel Méndez, OP, for his unpub-

lished thesis on the Delegates of the Word (2003, see n. 3). Miguel died very suddenly in 2008, at the young age of thirty-nine. He was the Novice Master of the Dominicans of Central America at the time of his death. In his honor, I dedicate this chapter to my dear brother and friend, *Miguelito*.

6. A number of the men who attended this first workshop in 1966 were part of a prayer apostolate called *Celadores del Apostolado de la Oración*—married men who visited the homes of Catholic families to pray the rosary before an image of the Sacred Heart of Jesus. It is very interesting to note that many of these same men were also leaders in the radio literacy program and the early peasant organizations. Cited from Miguel Méndez, OP, "Los Delegados de la Palabra de Dios," 29.

7. From an interview that Fr. Miguel Méndez, OP, had with Juan Bautista Mejía, one of the original seventeen Delegates of the Word of the diocese of Choluteca. Cited in Miguel Méndez, OP, "Los Delegados de la Palabra de Dios," 30; see also n. 29 in Méndez.

8. José Antonio Palacios, "La Celebración de la Palabra de Dios en Honduras" (Madrid: University of Salamanca, 1992, Anexo I). Cited in Miguel Méndez, OP, Los Delegados de la Palabra de Dios," 33.

9. Cristóbal Méndez was one of the early leaders of the movement of the Delegates of the Word in Honduras. After serving as a delegate for twenty-eight years, he entered the Dominican Order to become a preaching friar. Most recently, Cristóbal has served as pastor of the Achi-speaking Mayan indigenous community in Rabinal, Alta-Verapaz, Guatemala. The several quotes from Cristóbal that appear in this chapter are from a long letter that he recently wrote to me, sharing his memories of being a part of this historical movement. I am most grateful to Cristóbal for the generous sharing of his own experience. Here onward: Cristóbal Méndez, OP, letter to author.

10. *Pastoral Constitution on the Church in the Modern World*, http://www.vatican.va/archive/hist_councils/ii_vatican

_council/documents/vat-ii_const_19651207_gaudium-et-spes_en.html.

11. *The Constitution on the Sacred Liturgy,* http://www.vatican.va/archive/hist_councils/ii_vatican_council/documents/vat-ii_const_19631204_sacrosanctum-concilium_en.html.

12. Bro. Noe's words are engraved in my own heart, as I was one of his students of theology at the Superior Institute for Theological Studies (I.S.E.T.) in Lima, Perú in 1985. See also the CELAM Medellín Document: "The Church in the Present-Day Transformation of Latin America in Light of the Council," 6, 2.4.

13. Cristóbal Méndez, OP, letter to author.

14. Gustavo Blanco and Jaime Valverde, "Honduras, Iglesia y Cambio Social" (San José: DEI, 1987), 47; cited in Miguel Méndez, OP, 27. Some of the information on Monseñor Evelio Domínguez was found on the Internet: http://lavozdesuyapa.wordpress.com/inicio/.

15. This is the title that was finally agreed upon by the bishops for the new movement of lay preachers. And those who were delegated for this new ministry were called, almost from the beginning, "Delegates of the Word."

16. Miguel Méndez, OP, "Los Delegados de la Palabra de Dios," 53.

17. See the descriptions of the different *faces* of the Latin American and Caribbean Church in the CELAM Documents of Puebla (31–39, 234, 365, 1164) and Santo Domingo (30, 105, 137, 178–79, 299).

18. José María Tojeira, "Panorama Histórico de la Iglesia en Honduras" (Tegucigalpa: CEDOH, 1990), 217.

19. Mensaje Pastoral de los Obispos de Honduras, 1976, 5. Though the recognition of the Movement of the Celebration of the Word of God was not officially recognized as a ministry within the local Church until 1999, references to the ministry of the Delegates appear as early as this 1976 Pastoral Message from the bishops.

20. Ibid., 8.

21. Miguel Méndez, OP, "Los Delegados de la Palabra de Dios," 34, n.38.

22. Equipo de Promoción de Comunidades Cristianas, "El Hombre y el Trabajo," *Celebraciones Dominicales de la Palabra de Dios, para Adviento, Navidad y Epifanía*. Diocese of Choluteca, 1975, 3.

23. Equipo de Promoción de Comunidades Cristianas. "El Hombre y su Comunidad," *Celebraciones Dominicales de la Palabra de Dios, para tiempo de Pentecostés*. Diocese of Choluteca, 1975, 3.

24. Palacios, "La Celebración de la Palabra de Dios en Honduras," cited in Miguel Méndez, "Los Delegados de la Palabra de Dios," OP, 6.

25. Conferencia Episcopal de Honduras, "Mensaje Pastoral en ocasión del Décimo Aniversario de la Celebración de la Palabra de Dios." Title of the Pastoral Letter: "Ten Years along New Paths" (Tegucigalpa, 1976), 3, 6. Can also be found in the Boletín Eclesial de Honduras, No. 161, (July–Aug, 1976).

26. Cristóbal Méndez, OP, letter to author.

27. Ibid.

28. Parts of this section are taken from an earlier article: Brian J. Pierce, "Delegates of the Word: Lay Preaching in Honduras" *America* April 6, 1996, 14–17.

29. Ibid.

30. Blanco and Valverde, "Honduras, Iglesia y Cambio Social," 103–4; cited in Miguel Méndez, OP, "Los Delegados de la Palabra de Dios," 57.

31. Blanco and Valverde, "Honduras, Iglesia y Cambio Social," 138–9. Cited in Miguel Méndez, OP, "Los Delegados de la Palabra de Dios," 60.

32. Conferencia Episcopal de Honduras, 1976, "Mensaje Pastoral," 12–13.

33. *Día a Día con Monseñor Romero: Meditaciones para todo el Año*, (San Salvador: Archdiocese of San Salvador, 1999), 60. See other sources for Oscar Romero quotes: *Mons. Oscar A. Romero: Su Pensamiento; Mons. Oscar A. Romero: Su Diario*—a collection of his homilies and his diary (San

Salvador: Archdiocese of San Salvador, 2000); and James R. Brockman, SJ, compiler and trans., *The Church Is All of You* (Minneapolis: Winston Press, 1984); *The Violence of Love* (San Francisco: Harper and Row, 1988).

34. *Mons. Oscar A. Romero: Su Pensamiento*, Homily of August 20, 1978.

35. Ibid., Homily of February 18, 1979.

36. Cristóbal Méndez, OP, letter to author.

37. His Holiness Pope John Paul II, Homily in San Pedro Sula, Honduras, March 8, 1983 (from the Web site of the Holy See).

38. Ibid.

39. Ibid.

40. "La Iglesia y la Función del Delegado," *Boletín Nacional de la Celebración de la Palabra*, Año 2, (Tegucigalpa, December 1984), 14. Cited in Miguel Méndez, OP, "Los Delegados de la Palabra de Dios," 63.

41. After the year 2000, the number of delegates leveled off at approximately ten thousand.

42. Documentos Oficiales de Conferencia Episcopal de Honduras, vol. 4 (Tegucigalpa, 1991–1997), 51. Cited in Miguel Méndez, OP, "Los Delegados de la Palabra de Dios," 75.

43. These workshops, usually lasting four to five days, cover a wide spectrum of topics: Scripture, liturgy, sacraments, preaching, social doctrine of the Church, and so forth. Since the educational level of many of the Delegates is still rather low (although this is also changing), a popular methodology based on practical, catechetical, and pastoral formation is the norm.

44. 1991 Directory for the Celebration of the Word: *Mujeres en la Celebración de la Palabra*, 5.

45. Leticia Esperanza Pineda de Hércules, Delegate of the Word from the community of Los Almendros, Choloma, Honduras (email, November 2009).

46. Elías Ruiz, *El Astillero: Masacre y Justicia* (Tegucigalpa: Editorial Guaymuras, 1992), 6–17.

47. These words, though probably not 100 percent accurate, are drawn from the depths of my heart, where they were sown the day in 1992 that Don Felipe's son, Reinaldo, spoke them.

5

Brazil:
The Right of Communities
to a Full Christian Life

Nadir Rodrigues da Silva, OP

A GREAT ENIGMA SURROUNDS the Catholic Church in Brazil. On one hand, longtime observers are fully aware of the shortage of priests, especially in the highly publicized situations of the remote areas of the northern and northeastern regions of the country. Furthermore, many of the priests in these areas are foreigners. The shortage exists all over Brazil, however, and especially in the densely populated urban slums.

On the other hand, close observers, especially anthropologists, have been astonished by the vitality of the Catholic communities. Missionaries from other countries, even in regions in the south of Brazil, often compare Christian life in these communities with that of their own regions where there are more priests. And almost invariably they conclude that a greater presence of priests does not guarantee either the vitality of the life of faith or the existence of leaders with a Christian vision. On the contrary: when there are few priests, and where there is dynamic participation by community members, the result can be vibrant Christian communities led by wise local leaders, capable of authentically linking their faith with hope and charity—that is, making the connection between faith and social and political initiatives aimed at overcoming injustice and building a society in which human rights are guaranteed for all, a society in which all participate in the decisions that affect their lives.

Given the current situation, we will reflect in this chapter on two issues: First, why are there not enough priests in certain regions of Brazil? Second, how do communities without priests choose and prepare their leaders and deepen the living of their Christian faith?

A Church with Much Prayer and Few Masses

It is commonly suggested that the lack of Christian family formation is responsible for the shortage of vocations to the priesthood. Could it be that the Lord is not asked enough "to send workers into his vineyard"? Seemingly, this is not likely. After all, in parts of Brazil, priests are very highly regarded, and there is a strong desire for the celebration of the sacraments, which depends on the mediation of the priest. Thus the history of these communities needs to be investigated in order to uncover more objective explanations and thereby avoid moralistic conclusions based on judgments about people's faith or intentions.

The experience of living in the Christian communities of these northern Brazilian regions cannot be compared with that of European communities, or even with those established in areas where there are small property owners such as those of the European immigrants to southern Brazil. Equally different was the experience of communities formed by Italians and other Europeans who immigrated to replace the slaves, especially to the coffee plantations in the state of São Paulo.

The first Brazilian Christian communities were born of the contradictory path of Christianity itself, which arrived along with the European colonizer. This experience was marked by the discrimination of the powerful colonizer toward the others, be they poor Portuguese, indigenous, or, later on, black slaves—an experience stamped by a forceful exploitation of the Christian message and ecclesial structures in favor of colonial domination. Even in the churches special places were set aside for those who enjoyed the privileges of colonizers, who were almost always presented as people living exemplary Christian lives. The places left over were for the impoverished, who were maintained in their illiterate state, without rights and almost always treated as sinners. Where the slaves were large in numbers they had their own churches, which effectively separated them from "the whites and Christians." The indigenous people who had survived genocide and ethnocide were denied the right to exist as a separate people to such an extent that they never even had the chance to have separate places of worship.

In the emerging urban centers and even more so in the remote rural areas, there were few priests working among the most impoverished. Because of the system of ecclesiastical patronage, Catholicism was the official religion and the colonial state maintained the ecclesiastical institution. For this reason, the preaching and teaching of Christian doctrine was limited to the catechism and was carried out by priests belonging to religious congregations rather than by diocesan clergy. This would give rise to the marked devotions to the saints associated with these congregations. And because the priest was present only during the *desobrigas* (trips lasting months or even years and restricted almost exclusively to the celebration of the sacraments), especially in the more remote countryside, the practice of Christianity being learned was kept alive by prayer leaders, both men and women. As such, these poorly served remote communities applied what they learned to their daily lives and frequently combined this with the messages and rites present in the religious experience of blacks or indigenous people. It is worth keeping in mind that the use of Latin in eucharistic celebrations and other rituals introduced a mysterious element into the prayer experience, as people did not understand exactly what they were praying or singing.

This process brought about what has been called popular Catholicism, which is characterized fundamentally by a devotional religious life with much prayer and few Masses. The Eucharist and the other sacraments whose administration is reserved to priests were celebrated only when the priest was present; but there was a great deal of prayer, led by the prayer leaders; and there were also many fiestas organized by local communities.

Under these socioreligious circumstances, how could one expect certain young people to want to become priests or religious, and how could many parents encourage their children to do so when priests brought a message tainted with colonial domination? As such, in some communities, discrimination and prejudice were so deeply rooted that even the wish to become a priest could be interpreted within the community as an unbecoming ambition.

The experience of the communities of immigrants, who were almost exclusively of Italian origin in upstate São Paulo, was different but equally discouraging. With the exception of some anarchistic groups, the majority brought with them the traditional Catholic religious practices of their place of origin. These immigrants experienced problems from local, entrenched bosses who expressed their dominance by controlling the chapels and the priests who celebrated the sacraments there. Priests were guests of the "big house," that is, of the plantation mansions, homes of slave masters up to recent times. In contrast, the immigrants lived either in the places that had formerly been the *senzala*, the slave quarters, or in hastily constructed and miserable huts.

For many persons in northeastern regions, the landlords not only controlled the sacred space but also served as the patrons of religious fiestas, a role that linked them to the saints and led the priests to praise their "generosity" and other honorable qualities. In contrast, however, the priests directed their sermons toward the impoverished faithful, moralistically attributing their misery to a lack of Christian virtue and to fondness for drink and sexual disorders, and obliging them to obey their landlords and not to desire what belonged to their landlords if they wanted to be blessed by God.

In these circumstances, parents preferred to prevent their children from thinking of becoming priests, because they could not allow them to associate with or play into the hands of the landlords who mercilessly mistreated and exploited them.

On the other hand, the experience of these communities after the Proclamation of the Republic in 1889—a year after the promulgation of the law that abolished slavery—equally discouraged young men from joining the clergy. It should be remembered that the Catholic Church was part of a two-sided political movement, neither of which was favorable to the experience of Catholics at the grassroots level or to popular Catholicism. The first was aimed at restoring the privileges of the ecclesiastical patronage, which was lost upon the proclamation of the first Republican Constitution, which instituted the secularization of the state. The hierarchy insistently sought this restoration and partly succeeded in negotiations with Getúlio Vargas, who was president at the beginning of the 1930s, when Vargas recognized that Catholicism, although not the official state religion, was "the religion of Brazilians." The Christian communities neither participated in nor gained anything through this.

The other side of this movement was the "Romanization" of the Brazilian Catholic Church that was taking place throughout Catholicism during the nineteenth century and had great influence on the communities of popular Catholicism. How did this process come about?

Up to this time, the Brazilian Catholic Church had been institutionally fragile. It was not in the interests of the Portuguese Empire that it be strong. Using the power of patronage conceded by the Vatican and restored immediately after Independence, the state limited the flow of funds and was not interested in increasing the number of bishoprics. The Church had to conform to this arrangement. But because Catholicism was no longer a state religion, the Church would have to strengthen its organizational structure and its autonomous presence in society.

Given its fragility and lack of public funding, the hierarchy decided to ask the Vatican for help. The Vatican, in turn, interested in increasing its influence over the recently independent Brazilian Church and aware of its fragility, sought support. It appealed to both male and female religious congregations, whose numbers were then expanding in Europe, to take responsibility for mission areas in Brazil. Following on that, it increased the number of dioceses and archdioceses and nominated bishops attuned to the Vatican's policy.

This had an important influence on popular Catholicism, but did not solve the problem of the shortage of native priestly vocations. Within a short time, many religious priests arrived from abroad and religious women took on roles complementary to the priesthood. With the aim of consolidating and reinforcing pastoral work while at the same time increasing clerical control, the process was centralized by establishing parishes and dioceses and, where necessary, building chapels to gather distant communities together for worship conducted (and controlled) by the clergy.

The foreign missionaries brought with them devotions favored by each religious order and devotions promoted by the Vatican. These devotions represented an abstract spirituality disconnected from the daily life of the people; they included the Sacred Heart of Jesus, the Heart of Mary, and the European apparitions of Our Lady and saints unknown to Brazilian communities. Thus the Catholicism lived by the people clashed with the Catholicism brought by the new missionaries as the consequence of an instruction from the Vatican to fight the mixture of superstitions with Catholic beliefs, as well as the ignorance of local leaders.

Without going into further detail, this process alienated the official Church, which was endorsed by the Vatican and imported from outside, from the communities that maintained their religious faith through their own efforts. In turn, in the majority of cases, the new missionary priests were further alienated from the communities because they came with the support of the large landowners and were saying Masses in chapels on their plantations and large farms.

Again, it was hardly likely that parents would want one of their children to become a priest. For one thing, it no longer seemed necessary, since the Church appeared to be well supplied with personnel and funds from abroad. Worse still, it would mean that their son would have to ally himself with the opposition, the exploiters and masters. In any case, the foreigners deemed ordination of natives undesirable, since the faith of the natives was considered misguided and their religious practice that of ignorant people.

How Priestless Communities Came About

Beyond the colonial, post-Independence, and early republic periods, this shortage of priests continues even today. It has been exacerbated in recent years by a considerable reduction in the number of religious and priests in European countries and a consequent reduction in the number of missionaries. On the other hand, the priority given to forming priests in Brazil did not reach its objectives, and in many cases it generated more problems than solutions.

165

Numbers were often more important than the quality of formation or the motivation for the priestly mission.

But the communities, especially those that opted for evangelizing pastoral work to promote base Christian communities, organized themselves and learned to live their faith with a minimal presence of priests. They have a high regard for the Eucharist and the celebration of the other sacraments, but some sacraments (baptisms and marriages) began to be celebrated by lay ministers, and the Sunday celebration became a Celebration of the Word, with distribution of Communion, presided over by lay ministers. The presence of the priest, when he is able to visit the community, becomes a source of joy, but the Christian life of the community does not depend solely on him or on those sacraments over which only he can preside.

The decentralization of ministries helps the community to grow. The participation of women (religious, the young, or mothers of families), who are ineligible for ordination, is a striking characteristic of the communities. In order to prepare people for the different types of ministry and service, the communities have an ongoing process of formation and skill training. Teaching Bible circles (group study and reflection), which demands biblical formation, and the coordination of social pastoral work, which demands Christian spirituality and political awareness, are all opportunities for the formation of new leaders.

AN "EVANGELIZING CHURCH COMMUNITY"

In terms of concrete examples, it is worth highlighting two experiences of the diocese of Goiás (in the state of Goiás, Brazil) from 1970 onward. The starting point was the decision of the Dominican bishop, Dom Tomás Balduino, to reorganize his local church according to the inspiration and guidelines of the Second Vatican Council. First he generated a process of reflection and mobilization in the parishes in preparation for parish assemblies. These assemblies were opportunities for study and dialogue on the mission of the Church in the daily lives of the people, but also occasions on which the members democratically chose members for parish commissions and delegates for the diocesan assembly. With time, the diocese itself became a "church assembly," in which decisions were made by the participating Christians, so that the traditional centralization of power and mission in the figures of the bishop and his clergy were bypassed.

It was not easy to change what was considered "natural": the personal power of the bishop and the priest to make decisions on everything related to Christian life within their own territory. A broad program for leadership formation prepared community representatives for greater participation in decision making, and the effort was made to do everything through the medium of dialogue and from the wellsprings of a spirituality centered on the following of Jesus Christ, with the aim of creating evangelizing communities that would confirm Christ's message with example and word.

Leadership of Faith and Action

A decision was reached at the diocesan assembly to set up a team to take charge of the formation of leaders who would be capable of animating and renewing the life of the Church and who would work in the milieu in which they lived for the service of the impoverished. This was one way of living the option for the poor: following the example of Jesus in going out to meet the people in their daily lives; discovering their needs and their ways of facing them; inviting those interested to undertake skill-based formation to become better leaders; and providing formation that would overcome the passivity that had been promoted by the notion of the "faithful," so that leaders instead would become true friends and followers of Jesus, understanding all that the Father had revealed through his word and putting it into practice, and that the Church should make this revelation present in each time and place.

The process was not linear. The work became rooted better in some places than in others, either because of the priest's lack of willingness, vision, or conviction, or because of the type of reaction caused by the process. In a region of predominantly large landowners, for example, the immediate reaction was one of aggression, expressed through threats and persecution of the priests and new leaders; these large landowners could not understand or imagine that the Church would distance herself from their generosity or prefer the company of the poor, illiterate, ignorant, and handicapped. In other areas, where medium-sized holdings rented out to tenants (who pay half their crop as rent) predominated, the negative reaction was slower but no less violent. This violence was engendered by the fear that these tenants, who had become more aware of their rights and of the law, more knowledgeable, and more active participants in a Christianity concerned about every dimension of their lives, would begin to demand their rights to the land, thereby putting into practice what was defined in a law called the Land Statute.

It is worth remembering that all this took place at a particularly violent period during the military dictatorship that ruled Brazil between 1964 and 1985. Activism connected to workers' rights and, even more so, to the Popular Education movement (including efforts initiated by Paulo Freire) was easily branded as subversive activity. The local elites, the traditional masters, anxious to maintain their privileges, took advantage of this to put all the work of the Goiás diocese under suspicion.

The Itapuranga Experience

In some municipalities, such as Itapuranga, this process led to an increase in the number of base Christian communities, initially known as gospel groups. The process was started by a team from another region that had had a priest. There were more than forty thousand people living in the municipality, two-thirds of whom were in the countryside. Gradually, dialogue with the existing parish council led to the decision that more time should be given to pastoral care of communities in the rural areas. From then on, all the families were visited in every corner of the municipality. In addition to making direct contact with the families, the aim of the visit was to identify "born leaders"—trustworthy people who could take initiative in all aspects of life.

In a decentralized manner, groups of leaders appeared who were willing to join this formation process. It meant linking faith and life, following the practice of Jesus. For this reason, many meetings used the parable of the wheat and the darnel, but presented it as rice and *timbete*, in order to connect it with agriculture and the most obnoxious weed of the region. The parable led to a progressive reflection on reality that was later reinforced by other parables, but it always returned to the mission of continuing the evangelizing process begun by Jesus.

Encouraged to decide freely about how they felt called by God to live out the message of Jesus, some people preferred to animate the base Christian communities, while others preferred just to be part of the church community, working in the rural workers' union and in other organizations of the people. They gradually succeeded, for example, in electing union leaders committed to upholding the rights of farm laborers, the majority of whom were tenants.

It is important to be aware that the priest in this municipality and parish announced from the very first day that he did not intend to remain in the place for long. In dialogue with the community, during meetings to celebrate the Eucharist, the following objective was defined: in more or less three years, the community would have people prepared to assume all the services and ministries necessary to be an adult autonomous community not dependent on outside help.

At the end of the third year, leaders from all over the municipality, united in assembly, decided that they needed direct support for a further year so that the local community would feel up to working autonomously. The local elites decided to expel the pastoral team because they considered them subversive and responsible for the change in the popular vote in a local election. This had the effect of making the support of the pastoral team less direct and intense, so that the lay leaders, even amid increasing difficulties, had to take on practically all the services, except, of course, presiding at the eucharistic celebration and communal penance services, which were reserved exclusively for ordained ministers.

Consequently, diocesan officials considered taking the step of requesting permission from the Vatican to ordain people to assume functions that were otherwise exclusively reserved to the priest. But because this evangelizing work was provoking such tension and mistrust even among the Church hierarchy, which resulted in an official visitation from the Vatican, the diocese decided not to send the request to the Vatican, knowing that it would not be granted.

Hence, after a short time, a new priest took over the work of the parish and assumed the traditional form of organization and ecclesial animation. The local community did not have the possibility of seeing people of proven faith, who were already carrying out services and ministries in a limited form, being ordained to animate their Christian life to the full, including the celebration of the sacraments of the Eucharist and penance.

The Santa Fé Experience

The concrete experience of the Santa Fé community was profoundly marked by faith, fraternity, and shared responsibility.

In 1978 a group of Dominican sisters answered the call of Dom Tomás Balduíno, then Bishop of Goiás, to become part of the process of the commissioning of lay ministries in the diocese. The location chosen by the group, the town of Santa Fé de Goiás, which is inhabited by migrants from other states in Brazil, especially from the northeast, is now the center for attending to the basic needs of the surrounding small landholders and also functions as a centralizing nucleus for the groupings of these country people.

The sisters were warmly welcomed and, from the beginning, sought to become part of the community by forming relationships and creating neighborliness. Home visits, which brought about integration in both family and community spheres, also facilitated a mutual getting to know one another and winning of confidence. Above all, these visits confirmed for the families their feeling of being in control of the context they had created and were living out.

The truth of St. Vincent de Paul's observation that "the poor are our [lords and] masters" became evident for the sisters as they put down roots in the locality. As the village families and the groups scattered over the countryside, with their profound faith and fidelity to religious customs, they very naturally passed on their convictions and religious practices to the newer generations. Their faith is lived in intimacy with the Holy Trinity, with the Lord Jesus especially in his passion and cross, a familiarity with Our Lady through praying the rosary, the Gospel of the poor, and with the patron saints whose feasts are preceded by novenas (nine days of prayer). Serenades, invitations, and preparation for Christmas, wakes reuniting families as a member passes away to the afterlife: all of these are opportunities to experience and pass on the faith.

The *Folia de Reis e do Divino* (Festival of the Kings and of Pentecost) is also a real form of catechesis. With their hymns, dances, prayers, and special dress, they remember and celebrate moments of the life of Jesus. Processions through the streets, stopping from house to house, the *foliões* recall the journey of the magi to Bethlehem and conclude with the adoration of God Incarnate. The celebration culminates with a community fiesta and a generous meal provided by a family chosen in advance to welcome the group.

Lent is a time of penance, prayer, fasting, and good deeds. Prayerful processions with a cross at dawn in which all participate, adults and children alike, demonstrate their identification with the passion and death of Jesus.

The people catechize the children in their own way, living their faith with their practices and celebrations prepared in a biblical context, with a wealth of hymns, colors, sounds, and amazing creativity, in the simple moments of life.

In this context of intense living of piety, reverence for God, and fraternity with much prayer and few Masses, where do the sisters fit in?

Their aim, when they arrived in Sante Fé de Goiá, was simple: following the guidelines of the diocese, to make more explicit the gospel already present at the heart of the communities by sharing the life of the people. Thus they decided, first, to begin Bible study based on the parables with the already existing gospel groups, in order to help them to understand the new concept of the church, which is not a temple but a community. Second, they aimed to foster the formation of leaders by further developing natural aptitudes. Third, they encouraged the creation of ministries, not as an individualized power but as service to the life of the community. Fourth, they formed teams for ministerial service, decentralizing power and confirming the words of St.

Peter that "every Christian ought to witness to the hope that lives in his/her heart," as was expressed in song by a community member: "Every Christian should be a light, obeying the words of Jesus." Finally, they gradually tried to organize the community and thereby reaffirm the responsibility of the laity.

These initiatives were welcomed especially by the women who attended literacy classes with the hope of becoming gospel group coordinators and animators of the celebrations that were regarded as eucharistic moments. The religious and laity formed in this movement are delegated by the bishop to administer certain sacraments.

This Scripture-based formation led to awareness that the community can be an instrument of transformation, "so that all may have life and life to the full." So with the discovery of their rights, the women set up a very important association that became a "conversation circle" for discussing, deliberating about, and solving the problems of the people. At the same time, the Rural Workers' Unions, which are instrumental in improving and transforming workers' everyday lives, were founded.

Scripture-centered community formation has continued through prayer, organization meetings, and assemblies to evaluate and reinforce action and decision making, guaranteed by the conviction that it is their faith that leads them to struggle for a better life.

However, initially the acceptance of this religious work was not peaceful. The large landowners, an elite group that actively defends its own interests, saw these popular organizations as a threat to their objectives. They were troubled at the possibility of the growth and affirmation of a Church that is different and does not depend on them for resources and is independent of their political and social domination.

On the other hand, many pastoral workers who were foreign missionaries visiting Santa Fé recognized, in this community process, the promise of a church living the gospel. On one occasion, when the families were harvesting their corn together, they decided to organize a community *Pamonhada* (traditional regional corn harvest festival). At the end of the day, this festive meal became an opportunity for sharing among them the great variety of dishes that had been prepared. A young Canadian priest who was present declared that what had happened there enabled him to experience the real meaning of Eucharist.

The conviction that these people who accept responsibility and actively participate *are* the Church is reflected in what took place when the diocesan representatives spoke at the annual national meeting of base Christian communities. A woman tapped the bishop's shoulder and said, "This is Tomás Balduíno, the Bishop of *my* diocese."

The people use their creativity in the celebrations and in different events in the daily life of the community. During the novena in preparation for the patron saint's Feast, an illiterate farm laborer once expressed his feelings about the beauty of the celebration by bending down and raising his arms, saying, "Sister, I have been reborn today." "For me, the only thing better than this is heaven," exclaimed another farm laborer.

All processes are cyclical—"there is a time to seek and a time to lose, a time to mourn and a time to laugh"—but the people are aware that the flame lit by the gospel is for a lifetime. It is never quenched. With the passing of time, the journey of the people of God in Santa Fé was consolidated. The strength and determination of the women, associated in their work, living, sharing, and co-responsibility, are a guarantee that principles and practice, deepening of faith and celebration are passed on. The reception and integration of newly arrived families and new families being constituted by young people were guaranteed by the teams who were mindful of their role in developing this parish beyond traditional patterns.

In 2007 the community enthusiastically welcomed as their resident parish priest the pastor who was appointed to this parish. All were ready to continue collaborating to safeguard the decentralized character of the parish community and the lay people's right to authentic participation. As was to be expected, a change in the structure and method of evangelization took place. The lay people firmly and conscientiously sought to continue along the path that had already been forged, and when a tendency toward clerical imposition arose, they had their own ways of helping the young priest to keep alive the flame of the new way of being church.

Today things have changed. The religious sisters have moved on to another mission area due to specific circumstances within their own religious congregations, and there is a definite tendency toward a return to the former parish structure. Yet, if the flame continues to burn, it will be because the Spirit is present in the people, nourishing their dreams, sustaining their faith and hope, and leading them to discover their power and capacity to reinvent life in the newness of the gospel.

The proof that God's kingdom happens; the conviction that its presence is sacrament; the certainty that hope is sustained in simplicity and poverty, in faith, sharing, and living; and the fact that the people experience fully that the church is the Body of Christ, God's people, the baptized who are conscious of their mission to announce the good news of the kingdom—all these are considered positive points in this process of evangelization.

Similar experiences are to be found throughout Brazil and Latin America. How could one not recognize the power of the base Christian community encounters at local and national levels? In the context of a Charismatic Catholic

Church and the proliferation of Pentecostal churches, how can one not notice the gospel in the hands of communities searching for a new church, axis and compass for the world?

God willing, the Latin American laity's living out of the mission entrusted to them by the Lord, vitally renewed with Vatican II, Medellín, Puebla, and Santo Domingo, and officially confirmed at the Latin American Conference at Aparecida, São Paulo, a mission understood as participation in the mission of Christ, prophet, priest, and king, will be adopted and exercised by all the baptized.

6

Priestless Parishes: From Past Responses to Future Solutions

David Orique, OP

AFTER A LONG AND FRUITFUL LIFE as a Dominican priest and scholar, Fr. Edward Cleary's academic contributions had seemingly ended on that November day when he passed away peacefully in his room. However, in the subsequent weeks and months of sorting through his working papers generated by over fifty years of study in and on Latin America, I discovered a number of additional projects he had conceptualized as well as several that were partially completed; this book was one of them. Another project that he had begun would have been the crowning scholarly achievement of his life: the forthcoming *The Oxford Handbook of Christianity in Latin America.*

Throughout the twenty years in which I knew Ed and the eleven trips to Latin America with him, he demonstrated an indefatigable passion for the region and adhered to a disciplined work schedule—two qualities that we wish to promote to honor his memory, and to make known this fascinating and most Catholic region of the world. His choice of the chapter authors reflects both the breadth of his knowledge and the capaciousness of his collegiality. He cast a wide net, scholarly and geographically, to bring together those who would knowledgably treat the topic, as well as to bring their ideas to an English-speaking audience. The particular value of this collection is Ed's invitation of scholars actually on the ground. This reflected his strong empirical bent and his appreciation of first-hand experience in scholarship. He valued theoretical research balanced with practical understanding. He appreciated seeing, experiencing, watching, asking, and learning.

Professor Cleary's academic activities, professional pursuits, and prolific scholarship reflected his research interests and personal passion for Latin America—a lifelong passion that was ignited during his first assignment to Bolivia as a Dominican friar. As a social scientist, he regularly lectured, studied, researched, and published about Latin America, and especially on the subject of the Latin American Catholic Church. His interests ranged from politics and human rights to religious change and pluralism. *The Challenge of Priestless Parishes* continues Dr. Cleary's study of the changing religious landscape in the Latin American Church.

This concluding chapter of the book presents an overview of the different ways in which Catholicism survived in five selected regions, although there were other countries and areas that might have been considered. Nevertheless, this final chapter offers a chronological outline of the diverse responses of the laity and clergy to the shortage or absence of the ordained that was, for the most part, common to the whole of Latin America. This chronological synopsis of the responses of the laity to the shortage of priests begins with the colonial period, followed by the independence era and the twentieth-century developments, and culminating in the twenty-first century. To provide some sense of the historical reasons for the paucity of clergy, this segment of this concluding chapter offers readers a sense of the sweep of events and circumstances that have influenced the development of Catholicism with a scarcity of clergy. While, for heuristic reasons, this chapter also makes distinctions between the Church as a centralized hierarchical institution and the Church as the grassroots community of believers, in reality all are the one people of God—and, also in reality, tensions can exist and have existed between the Church as clergy and the Church as laity. This chapter concludes with a thematic summary of possible solutions to the situation of the Church without priests that were derived from the laity's responses in the course of the histories of the selected regions. This thematic summary suggests what can be learned by laity and clergy of the Church from the different expressions of Catholicism that the laity generated in the selected regions both with and without the support of the institutional Church. Lessons garnered from the responses to the lack or absence of priests ranged from home-based faith formation and living, to lessons learned from Catholic activism in the public sphere, to the inestimable guidance of the Spirit of God, and the consequent need for awareness, acknowledgment, and appreciation of full lay participation in the Christian life. These kinds of solutions offer some initial answers to the central question that Ed Cleary proposed: How did Catholicism survive in Latin America during long periods with a paucity of clergy? Recognizing that the initial answers generated in this concluding chapter require additional scholarly exploration, let us turn our attention to what took place during long periods of Latin American Church history.

A Short History of the Shortage

In the colonial period, the Church, which eventually included European, indigenous, and African peoples as well as their "pure" and mixed descendants, experienced both maldistribution and shortage of clergy. The general distribution of priests, after the initial arrival of clerics with the conquistadors, colonizers, and bureaucrats, consisted of religious priests ministering predominantly to large geographically dispersed rural populations in less lucrative regions and frontier zones, and diocesan priests serving mainly in densely populated, Europeanized, and more financially remunerative urban centers and their surrounding areas. To accompany and support the clergy's preaching of orthodox Christian doctrine, the institutional Church established dioceses with parishes, known as *doctrinas*, in indigenous towns; after the initial creation of the diocese of Santo Domingo in 1511, this kind of ecclesial organization extended into the Caribbean, then into Mexico in the 1530s, and into Peru after 1570.

The shortage of clergy to minister regularly and adequately to the growing rural populations as well as to the expanding urban poor directly contributed to the emergence of popular religion in Latin American Catholicism. One of the characteristics of the colonized indigenous peoples' conversion to Christianity was the acceptance of a Christian notion of God and the reception of the rite of baptism; the assumption or admission of the principal gods and rituals of the dominant group resonated with the various indigenous religious traditions. As such, while their religiosity was syncretic, many of the neophytes' beliefs and practices remained unchanged. The contributors to the present book pinpoint some of the early colonial manifestations of this folk Catholicism. Bruce Calder calls attention to the original incomplete evangelization as well as to the establishment of medieval Spanish *cofradías* (lay Catholic brotherhoods who venerated a particular saint) in early colonial *doctrinas* and parishes, which affected the development of popular religion among the Maya in Guatemala. Nadir Rodrigues da Silva asserts that Christianity was kept alive in Brazil by the prayer leaders and fiestas of popular religion. Cynthia Folquer focuses on the diversity of the expression of popular religion in Argentina, where three religious worlds—Spanish Catholicism, African traditions, and indigenous beliefs and rites—intermingled as people continued to call on the Andean gods of nature, Pachamama and Llastay, combined All Souls Day rituals with their cult of the dead, and frequented grottos erected as sacred spaces reminiscent of the shrines of their Inca conquerors. Brian Pierce highlights the seeds of Christianity sown by the labors of Bartolomé de Las Casas, Bishop of Chiapas, and the martyrdom of Valdivieso, Bishop of Nicaragua, that constituted the heralding of a Church both *of* and *for* the poor—a Church built on grassroots Catholicism. Edward Cleary points out that the grassroots people in Puerto Rico were "in control of the practice of Catholicism...in the domain of popular religion."

In the independence period, after three centuries of what Pierce denominates as the "shackles of centuries of colonialism," the Church, as part of the state apparatus and the recipient of ecclesiastical patronage, had become in most regions, as Calder noted about Guatemala, a "large, wealthy, and influential institution." In the 1800s, revolutionary events and processes accompanied and followed the different trajectories that regions took to break with their Iberian past by achieving independence and to generate state structures compatible with Enlightenment ideology. How Catholicism fared during the nineteenth century and beyond depended greatly on church-state relations and on whether the Church was perceived as a vehicle or obstacle to positivistic order and social progress.

While concordats with Rome set the parameters of rights and responsibilities of both parties for the growth of the institutional Church as the preferred religion, anticlerical liberal regimes championed religious freedom, seeking to curb Church control of, for example, education as well as to expropriate Church properties. Given that the papacy had initially denounced the revolution movements in Latin America, liberal and conservative governments of the new republics experienced contentious relationships with Rome. For example, as Folquer points out, after Argentina gained independence in 1810, this new nation's subsequent request for concordat with the papacy was never granted. Furthermore, although the Church received public funds to develop "romanized" diocesan and parochial structures to facilitate evangelization and catechesis, these organizational structures and activities generally did not extend to the scattered rural grassroots Catholics living in the interior. Indeed, given that both liberals and conservatives came from the upper classes, neither state nor Church furthered the interests of the majority of the population—those who were poor and oppressed. Consequently, the result—for example, in Argentina—was that popular religion, initiated during the colonial era, continued to characterize grassroots Catholicism in these virtually priestless regions.

The paucity and inconsistency of outreach to the masses in Latin America was further compounded by division among the clergy as most bishops and priests colluded with conservatives, while some "lower-class" clergy embraced the liberal platform. For example, in Brazil, where the Catholic Church lacked organizational, political, and economic influence at the time of Brazil's Independence in 1822, a strong centralized organizational structure increased clerical control, and great political influence developed by the time Brazil became a republic in 1889. Silva credits this to the Church's alignment with the powerful, which—in turn—also alienated grassroots Christians and created stark conditions of the Church at the local level both organizationally and pastorally. With fewer priests and less frequent visits to rural areas as well as lax clerical discipline (which further alienated the faithful), grassroots religious expressions became predominantly devotional. In Guatemala, where the independence won in 1821 changed little for the Maya, who constituted 70 percent of the population, indigenous communities relied on centuries-old institutions such as the cargo system, sodalities, and *cofradías* to lead and nurture their religious life. This religious tradition of the Maya served to maintain (an albeit syncretic) Catholicism in spite of the anticlerical measures of liberal regimes (beginning in 1873 and continuing until 1954) that relentlessly impoverished the Guatemalan Church and severely reduced its clerical workforce. As Calder contends, the Church in this eighty-year period constituted "a prime example of Latin America's experience of Catholicism without priests."

The shortage of priests also characterized nineteenth-century Christianity in the other new republics of the region—El Salvador, Nicaragua, Honduras, and Costa Rica, which (along with Guatemala) temporarily (1824–1840) functioned as the United Provinces of Central America. This federal republic promoted liberal reforms to end the Church's power, to institute religious freedom (and consequently, to welcome Protestant missionaries), and to divide society into a Creole upper class and an indigenous lower class. While these factors shaped the subsequent independent revolutionary governments, the histories of their church-state relations are unique. Costa Rica's anticlerical government maintained cordial church-state relations. El Salvador imitated Guatemala in its anticlericalism and its pro-Protestant stance. Conservative governments in Honduras and Nicaragua were generally supportive of the Church, although their liberal regimes did call for the expulsion of foreign priests, confiscation of Church property, and abolition of the tithe.

Meanwhile, in Puerto Rico, whose desire for freedom from Spanish domination was partially realized in 1898 when the territory was ceded to the United States during the Spanish-American war, the Church of the 1890s was, as

183

Cleary contends, "a ramshackle institution on a largely impoverished island." The glaring paucity of native clergy and insufficient efforts to recruit native candidates, coupled with the fact that more than half of the parishes were priestless as well as with the perception that its Spanish clergy were aligned with Spain against the people, had created a Church that was unwilling or unable to meet the pastoral needs of the grassroots. The situation was exacerbated by the large exodus of Spanish priests after the takeover by the United States and the subsequent overt arrival in droves of no-longer-prohibited Protestant missionaries and churches. As in the new republics of Latin America, declarations of religious freedom and the decline in the numbers of Catholic clergy left the mission field open to Protestant denominations, many of which were actively recruited by some of the liberal regimes. Fearful that their children would join Protestant groups, grassroots Catholics in Puerto Rico launched a counteroffensive, one of which was the lay-initiated response of the Hermanos Cheos.

In the twentieth century, one of the responses of the Latin American Church to the situation of priestless Catholic parishes consisted of the promotion of lay movements to undertake the tasks of evangelization, catechesis, and liberating action. In the mountainous central portion of Puerto Rico, the Hermanos Cheos assumed teaching and preaching roles normally reserved for the clergy. In the remote mountain areas of northwest Argentina, the deeply culture-embedded syncretic faith was maintained and transmitted by women who functioned as maternal authorities and *rezadoras* in their families and villages, and who spontaneously served as lay ministers in the Church. In the diocese of Goías in north-northeastern Brazil, grassroots base Christian communities (also called gospel or Bible study groups) evolved and increased in number; Bishop Balduino reorganized the local church-generated parish (and diocesan) assemblies' leadership teams of lay ministers, and commissioned the Catholic laity to conduct the Liturgy of the Word and to shoulder their responsibility as Christians in their common struggles for a better life. In urban and rural centers in Guatemala, European-initiated lay organizations such as Catholic Action contributed to the development of orthodox Christianity especially in rural areas, as did JOC and other lay catechists; these lay ministries in tandem with other popular organizations such as JEC, JUCA, and ACRO also advocated for causes close to the Church in the political realm, such as poverty, workers' rights, and land ownership. In the southernmost and northernmost prelatures of Honduras, Lay Delegates—and the transformed mayordomos—emerged as a new lay preaching movement whose catechetical, pastoral, and practical formation, along with regularly available Catholic radio broadcasts, equipped them to rejuvenate the local communities by ongoing systematic catechesis, with pastoral priority accorded the celebration of the Liturgy of the Word, and with prayerful application of Scripture to action in their historical reality. As such, these apostolic workers became the vital ministerial base through which, as Pierce asserts, "the local Church [in Honduras] truly became more and more...local."

Several kinds of societal and ecclesial developments contextualized twentieth-century explicit and implicit responses of Catholic laity to the shortage of priests. On the one hand, societal events and circumstances, for example, in the form of the landowners' resistance in Brazil, of the "baptism by fire" in Honduras, of the thirty-six-year internal conflict in Guatemala between leftist insurgents and the military, and of civil wars in Nicaragua and El Salvador, resulted in the persecution and/or massacre of many ordained and lay Catholics who were engaged in local and national struggles for justice for the poor. On the other hand, the mandate of John XXIII in 1963 that the North

American Church send 10 percent of their priests and sisters to Latin America resulted in an influx of foreign church workers to reestablish sacramental ministries in remote and priestless areas and to reinvigorate pastoral labors. Subsequently, Vatican II explicitly empowered the laity to take responsibility for the practice and extension of the faith, and the 1968 meeting of CELAM at Medellín committed the Latin American institutional Church to labor with the laity for the transformation of contemporary historical realities by its preferential option for the poor—an orientation for which, as Pierce points out, Bartolomé de Las Casas was an early architect already in the sixteenth century. CELAM's subsequent contentious meeting of conservative and progressive bishops at Puebla (1979) preceded John Paul II's caution about politicization of base Christian communities and the Vatican's questioning of liberation theology in the mid-1980s. At that same time, the revised Code of Canon Law included the directive (Canon 517.2) that, "due to a dearth of priests," the nonordained (that is, the laity) may be entrusted with the pastoral care of a parish. While the CELAM meeting in Santo Domingo (1992) debated the need for more centralized and hierarchical church structures as well as for less social activism, the assembled bishops agreed that needed new evangelization must be carried out by lay and ordained Catholics and must include issues of justice and liberation. At the Aparecida meeting (2007), after a detailed analysis of the challenges that faced the Church in Latin America, the bishops promised to renew ecclesial communities and pastoral structures.

This brief chronology of responses to the events and circumstances that seemingly caused a shortage of priests in the regions addressed in this book will now be followed by a presentation of the solutions taken by the Church as a centralized hierarchical institution and by the Church as a local community of faith.

The initial response of the institutional Church was to import diocesan and religious priests from foreign countries. As time passed, the Church also called for increased and more aggressive vocation promotion, including among local young adults, better seminary training for candidates to the priestly life, and more faithful living of the clerical state in public and private—approaches that continue to be pursued today. Additionally, in the United States, some converted Protestant ministers have been ordained, and ongoing discussion takes place in broad circles about the possibility of married clergy and of expanded roles of women. Indeed, in Brazil, the bishop's reorganization of the Goiás diocese included plans (that were never executed) to request Rome's permission to ordain "people of proven faith," that is, the lay leaders. Another response of the institutional Church pertained to increasing centralization through the establishment of new parishes, dioceses, and seminaries. Today, however, many U.S. dioceses are also closing, merging, or restructuring parishes to alleviate the shortage. Another response consisted of asserting hierarchical authority in the form of papal and episcopal directives about the sacramental and pastoral functions of the ordained, and about the desired evangelizing and catechetical activities of the laity as well as their involvement in "political" affairs. In accord with such directives, the institutional Church developed lay ministries by importing European lay Catholic organizations such as Catholic Action and movements such as the *Cursillos de Cristiandad* and the Catholic Charismatic Renewal. Such ecclesial lay ministries expanded when programs such as the Hermanos Cheos and the Delegates of the Word became official lay ministries in the Church. This recognition and development of lay ministries laid the groundwork for the collaboration of laity and clergy in what Samuel Ruíz, bishop of Chiapas, would denominate as a *pastoral de conjunto*. In their responses to the signs of their times, some ordained personnel of the institutional Church took progressive, others conservative, positions. For example, in Latin America, the conservative approach curbed the prominence of the progressive theology of liberation. While throughout the Church's history the faith community has coped with the ongoing problem of a divided clergy, perhaps the most severe division is experienced in China, where the so-called "official" Church—meaning the state-sanctioned Chinese Patriotic Catholic Association—rejects Vatican authority and appoints its own episcopacy.

The responses of the Church as a community of believers intent on deepening and living the faith at the local level pertains ultimately to baptism, the portal of the Church. This first sacrament of initiation into the life of the Church invites the baptized to share in the threefold mystery of Christ as priest, prophet, and sovereign—a mystery that is mirrored in the life of the Church and that calls the baptized to be priest, prophet, and sovereign within and beyond their local communities. To be priest is to heal, reconcile, and sanctify—as did *rezadoras* as they nurtured and transmitted the faith to their families and neighborhoods; to be prophet is to proclaim God's reign, word, and work—as did Delegates of the Word and others when they presided at the Liturgy of the Word and applied this word in their community's struggle for justice; to be sovereign is to serve, especially by participating through Catholic lay leadership in the governance of society and Church—as did the leadership teams and grassroots who participated in Brazil's decentralized and democratized ecclesial structures (assemblies) at parish, diocesan, and national levels, or as did those who demanded worker rights in Guatemala.

Practices for the Practical

The experiences of these selected regions of Latin America in dealing with a shortage of clergy contain useful practical lessons. Some lessons pertain to the way in which affected rural and urban lay populations responded to the twofold call of the Church to holiness and mission.

One such lesson pertains to inculturation, given that popular religion abounded (and abounds even today) in syncretic mixtures of Catholic tradition and ancestral religiosity as well as in home-based devotional practices and community-wide religious celebrations. From this, we learn the importance of welcoming and inculturating the faith in contemporary expressions of religiosity, for example, in Catholic Latino and Asian homes, parishes, and populations in the United States. As Folquer suggests, Christians might also learn from popular religions, such as the Amerindian Catholicism of northern Argentina, how to sacralize everyday space, how to care for the earth, how to develop a cosmovision that establishes links between the human and the divine Other, and how to mediate this spiritual relationship in processions, in blessings with holy water, in worshiping movements, and in remembering the dead.

Another lesson pertains to the importance of primary relationships and derives from the way in which priestless regions maintained, deepened, and lived the faith by membership in small gatherings, such as Bible study groups and base Christian communities. Through their regularly scheduled meetings, members of these groupings learned about, reflected with, and supported one another. As such, their faith-related needs for prayer and praise, as well as for catechesis and revitalization, were met in the cradle of supportive primary relationships. Similarly, the local religious processions of the Amerindians conveyed a sense of belonging, identity, intimacy, and equality that they sought to share by drumming to attract neighbors to join them. The salience of the underlying solidarity experienced in such faith-sharing groups and gatherings (and that frequently motivated their joining in the first place) needs consideration when envisioning local, parish, or diocesan revitalization programs, especially today where parish mergers and closures have resulted in the loss of primary relationships. Additionally, as Silva points out, several important pillars should anchor such groups in their communities, namely, neighborliness, hospitality, common meals, and visitation ministry, which together constitute the new prophetic act for today's world: the encountering of the Other.

Predating and precursoring the specific primary group developments was the long tradition of "pray-ers" in the domestic sphere. "Pray-ers" in the intimacy of the home, or designated "official pray-ers" in the community, kept alive and applied the Christianity they learned through devotional practices and homiletic messages rooted in their faith. An obvious lesson offered by this tradition is the importance of nurturing both knowledge and practice of the faith on a daily basis in home and neighborhood.

Other lessons pertain to the domestic sphere and, in particular, to women and youth. From the regional accounts, we also learned, not surprisingly, that women were the predominant "pray-ers" and prayer leaders in the family and the community; they were the principal educators and transmitters of religious knowledge and practice. Even base Christian communities strikingly reflected this "feminine genealogy" of grandmothers, mothers, and daughters creating and re-creating life as lay Christians called to holiness and mission. Indeed, what permeates the laity's responses to the shortage of priests is the pervasive presence and fundamental role of women in the various expressions of Catholicism presented. Accordingly, outside the home and neighborhood, women also participated in lay pastoral labors—including in teaching and preaching roles. For example, some women excelled as Hermanas Cheas; others served as Delegates of the Word; others participated at every level of Brazil's intra-ecclesial assemblies as well as in Guatemala's diverse lay Catholic organizations. (Although not mentioned, noteworthy was the strength and persistence of Guatemalan indigenous women, who, motivated by faith, struggled for justice and healing during Guatemala's conflictive history from 1954 to the present.) The lesson is that women share the same capacity for apostolic work as do men. As such, subtle and enduring patriarchal assumptions need to be reexamined and rectified, including the Latin American tendency of men to view religion as solely the arena of women and children. Moreover, the invisible glass ceiling over women, which limits their charisms and gifts, must be removed, so that they might have a more active voice and more equal participation in the public sphere and in the institutional Church. In like manner, lessons garnered from the regional accounts include the invitation to the local Church to reach out to and listen to youth, for the Spirit also speaks through their generation, as was done, for example, in the calls to ministries given the youthful Brothers Cheos, the young Guatemalan students and workers, and the teenage peasants who became Delegates of the Word.

Lessons can also be gleaned from the examples of responsible lay leadership, teamwork, and episcopal support of Catholic activism in the public sphere. As the Catholic organizations and movements extended more into the public sphere, they addressed social questions of a cultural, political, and economic nature. This Christian activism, whether initiated by laity or clerics and whether supported or not by ecclesial authorities, constituted a faith-based grassroots response to the mandate to proclaim the good news and to participate in the struggle for justice—for right relationship with God, with others, and with the rest of creation.

Consider the grassroots response to inroads in Puerto Rico by Protestant denominations and secular United States culture. In their response, the Hermanos Cheos inaugurated a vast but coherent and effective rural movement (with little support from the institutional Church) dedicated to evangelization, conversion, and reconstruction of Latin American Catholic culture. They were pioneers and prophets: they assumed teaching and preaching roles; they created the chapel system as an innovative and supportive link to distant parishes and as alternative congregational pilgrim centers for the periodic celebration (when possible) of Eucharist and the sacraments; as such, they maintained existing belief systems and religious practices of the Catholic culture.

Consider how, in like manner—but with ecclesiastical approbation and support from the onset—Catholic Action teams and catechists in Guatemala also labored to establish Catholic culture in rural areas governed by *cofradías* and Mayan *costumbres*, and/or infiltrated by Protestantism. The effective see-judge-act methodology of Catholic Action gradually extended to the revitalization of urban Christian family life and to the emergence of public-sphere involvements within base Christian communities. Concomitantly, rural workers and students (in ACRO, JOC, JEC, and JUCA) focused on re-Christianization and on justice for the poor. In the subsequent long and complex trajectory of political, economic, and military developments and tragedies in twentieth-century Guatemala and, most crucially, during the thirty-six years of internal armed conflict that generated violent repression by Guatemalan security forces (along with countless kidnappings and killings, as well as torture and rape of Catholic activists, and the "scorch and burn" eradication of noncombatant peasant populations), the shortage of clerics increased as many priests were exiled or murdered. Bishops responded by delegating lay workers to baptize, witness marriages, and conduct communion services; laity responded through the

Cursillo and Charismatic movements and the growing of base Christian communities. After Vatican II, fortified with the teachings of the Council, the preferential option for the poor of Medellín, and liberation theology as a foundation for Catholic social action, the laity and clergy eventually reconstructed the Church in Guatemala.

Consider as well the circumstances surrounding the development of Delegates of the Word in Honduras, which constituted another example of the empowering of the poor and often illiterate grassroots laity by the post–Vatican II episcopacy. Would-be delegates were trained with the needed pastoral skills and radio technology to enable them to take responsibility in their local communities for teaching and preaching, and, most distinctively, for presiding at the Liturgy of the Word. Together with Catholic organizations imported from other Central American countries as well as with base Christian communities, the delegates sought to transform social realities from the perspective of the gospel and in accord with the Church's option for the poor. In this pursuit, they too encountered challenges in the form of resistance from powerful farmers and ranchers as well as a "baptism by fire" from the shootings and massacres. Yet, they continued as the Church—a Church becoming more and more local as laity became active respondents to the call to holiness and mission, rather than distant and passive recipients of European colonial religiosity.

Finally, consider the lay responsibility that also developed in the wake of Vatican II in the Brazilian diocese of Goiás and that benefited from Paulo Freire's conscientization movement pertaining to popular education. Here, the arenas of pastoral ministry assumed by the laity consisted of networks of primary relationships to link life and faith, and extended from women's "conversation circles" and Bible study groups to base Christian communities and to lay ministers for the Liturgy of the Word and communion services.

Programs undertaken for outreach and formation also identified leaders by direct contact with and involvement of families, and established leadership training of grassroots peoples to prepare them to serve at all three levels of the intra-ecclesial assemblies. These parish, diocesan, and national assemblies of laity, who consistently dialogued on the Church's mission in daily living, clearly understood that they were called to share by virtue of their baptism in the mission of Jesus Christ, priest, prophet, and sovereign. Most significantly, as in Brazil, in carrying out their responsibilities they functioned as teams; they also democratically elected the members of parish commissions and their representatives to diocesan and national gatherings. Many, in union with their bishop, even envisioned the ordination of "people of proven faith" to fulfill the right of communities to the fullness of sacramental Christian life. In their service, they lived out the "option for the poor" and labored to address their needs through Catholic activism that supported workers' rights and organizations, tenant rights and land issues—including those of small landowners. As in many Latin American countries, their efforts in the struggle for justice met with opposition.

Two major kinds of lessons derived from these regional narratives pertain to the functioning of the Church at the grassroots level in the public sphere. The first lesson pertains to the need to build a solid foundation of networks of groups, organizations, and communities rooted in the Christian culture whose participants respond faithfully to the daily call to holiness. This sacred call requires the availability of ongoing programs of evangelization, catechesis, and even revitalization. From this cradle of primary relationships, the call to mission is actualized by the participants' experience of and informed reflection on their reality, and by their committed action to meet pastoral needs as well as to struggle for justice. Leaders need to be identified and their charisms welcomed. The lesson is clear: the mission of the Church can continue even with a paucity of clergy, when divine will converges with human determination of responsible lay leadership.

The second major lesson pertains to the diverse kinds of participation of the laity in the local Church to both facilitate and guarantee opportunities to exercise their right and responsibility to witness and proclaim the good news and to contribute through leadership to the governance of Church and society. Toward this end and in accord with the doctrine of subsidiarity, laity should participate in decision making at least at the local level. In accord with the equality of all human beings, decentralized structures and representative methods would more fully incorporate the laity's gifts and charisms. Finally, ministries tend to be most effectively carried out by teams of lay ministers in collaboration with the clergy—that is, in a *pastoral de conjunto.*

In addition to these lessons with respect to the public sphere, the issue of financial support also surfaced peripherally in the regional accounts and may be a contributing factor in the shortage of priests. For example, although the Guatemalan Church, as Calder states, now produces its own priests and exports priests to other countries, the shortage of clerics still continues. This is exemplified in the situation of three priests in 2009 in Panajachel who served fifty-six chapels and churches, which required that each cleric traveled to at least eighteen locales every week to celebrate the Eucharist with the laity. Why, then, do some Guatemalan priests leave their native land to minister in other countries? An answer may be found in one of the reasons why some Honduran Delegates left the lay ministry: lacking financial support for their labors of teaching and preaching, they were forced to seek remunerative work—to take a job in the secular world in order to earn a living.

The primary lesson to be learned from the regional accounts in this book, however, is openness to the Spirit of

God. The response of lay Catholics in these Latin American regions requires recognition of their various gifts and charisms as the workings of the Holy Spirit. In these local communities, there was a movement of something or Someone greater—of grace and/or the Holy Spirit—that sustained and strengthened the laity in their faith during the absence or shortage of clerical personnel. Accordingly, fortified by grace and moved by the Spirit, lay people recognized needs and assumed leadership in a variety of ways in their communities that met unfulfilled spiritual necessities.

Consider how the work of the Spirit was discernible in the strikingly spontaneous character of their lay vocations. In Puerto Rico, the Hermanos Cheos responded on their own—and surely with the guidance of the Spirit—to the undesired entrance of Protestantism and the unexpected exodus of Spanish priests. As deeply concerned and committed lay Catholics and not people aspiring to ordination they took up the task of revitalizing the Catholic faith and of shepherding the grassroots in the baptismal call to holiness and mission. In Argentina, the movement of the Spirit also generated spontaneous lay ministries. In Guatemala, the prompting of the Spirit was uniquely manifested in the spontaneous and rapid growth, among others, of the imported Charismatic movement. In Honduras, the Spirit prompted seventeen campesinos to approach their bishop with their communities' pastoral needs. The bishop was also led by the Spirit to form and commission these peasants as Delegates of the Word. As their ministry expanded, these lay leaders were even led to stand up (and sometimes to die) for the sake of justice, as Pierce reports. Indeed, in their teaching and preaching, these lay leaders experienced the presence of the Spirit of God, which one of the delegates maintained was "a voice within" her, such that, as she contended, "It is not I who speak, but God who gives me the words so that others can feel strengthened by God's Word."

In Brazil, the movement of the Spirit became an instrument of transformation as lay assemblies at local, diocesan, and national levels formed what truly represented the grassroots as the Church. Silva captures this movement of the Spirit when she writes:

> If the flame…of a new way of being Church…continues to burn, it will be because the Spirit is present in the people, nourishing their dreams, sustaining their faith and hope, and leading them to discover their power and capacity to reinvent life in the newness of the Gospel.

Accompanying the movements of the Spirit and the free-will responses of the laity to participate in needed pastoral labors was the clerical response from the institutional Church, as exemplified in the willingness and responses of many priests and bishops to support these endeavors and to facilitate, where possible, a *pastoral de conjunto*. In 2004, Pope John Paul II acknowledged the ever-present promptings of the Spirit in the Church and affirmed the need to foster shared responsibility between laity and clergy for the life and mission of the Church. He called on bishops to develop the needed structures of interaction and participation in the local Church that would make possible this shared responsibility.

This working of the Spirit both in the Church as the local community of believers and as the centralized hierarchical institution also invites recognition of the Church principle known as the *sensus fidelium* (sense of the faithful), to which John Paul II also alluded. Arguably, this sense of the faithful clearly spoke in the diversity of faith-filled responses of the communities sampled as they contended with the absence or shortage of priests. This sense of the faithful spoke in the lives of these people who lived and expressed an active belief in Jesus Christ. This sense of the faithful spoke in their concrete teaching and preaching, in their demonstrative acting and tangible advocating, as well as in their ordinary and extraordinary moments of fidelity to what was left to them—to what spoke to their hearts and minds, to what called them to build the reign of God now and to prepare for the one to come. Cleary speaks to this *sensus fidelium* when he says: "The baptized have the gift of the Holy Spirit that allows them to judge whether the message being preached is the Word of God that demands their assent or whether the message is not the Word of God." In each of the examples from this book, this statement seems to ring true. Would it ring true for the countless other communities around the world without ordained clergy? Most likely, because the communities studied met a deep and enduring human need: the need for guidance from the ever-present promptings of the Spirit working in them individually and collectively toward a deeper relationship with God, neighbor, and the rest of creation.

Moreover and most importantly, the celebration of the Eucharist in Catholic Christian understanding is central to sustaining and deepening the work of the Spirit in the individual and in the community. The Second Vatican Council reaffirmed and expanded this theological understanding by its statement that the Eucharist was "the source and summit" of Christian living (*Lumen Gentium* 11). Since the Christian life is both spiritual and physical because we live in time and prepare for eternity, Christians have a right to the Eucharist. Therefore, the existence of communities that lack the regular availability of priests and, consequently, of the Eucharist raises the question of how the celebration of this central rite of the Catholic tradition might be made available to all the faithful. In Latin America as well as in other places, some of the ways in which sharing in the Eucharist has been maintained in remote areas, and/or where there is a shortage or an absence of clergy, has been through the ordination of more deacons to offer communion services or Liturgy of the Word celebrations, although this is more common in the United States. Using hosts that were previously consecrated by an ordained priest at a Mass celebrated in another gathering of the Christian community, communion services permit reading of the word and reception of consecrated hosts. The Liturgy of the Word celebration is just that, a celebration of the word in Scripture without the reception of the Eucharist. This is not enough. Not only do these Christian communities have a high regard for the sacrament of the Eucharist and the other sacraments, they have a right, as Silva explicates, to a full sacramental Christian life—including the celebration of the Eucharist. So the question still remains: how might the Eucharist be made more available to all Catholics?

This question awaits response from the institutional Church. The Church, as the grassroots community of believers, has spoken and continues to speak. The Church, as the long neglected and institutionally underserved communities, continues to desire to share equally in dignity as Christians, regardless of their nationality, race, social status, gender, sexual orientation, and language. As the Church globally experiences the challenges and changes of the twenty-first century, such as the increasing effects of globalization and growing urbanization, as well as the expanding roles of women and pluralizing religious "markets," among other developments, Catholic Christianity will likely continue to face situations without clergy.

Perhaps by considering more deeply the Church life beyond our own limited purview, by viewing more globally the multitude of faith communities in other places, by contemplating more historically how the people of God (Church as institution and as local community) have functioned, we might benefit from the complexities and contradictions as well as the potentialities and possibilities of the universal faith community. Doing so might help us through the Spirit to discern ways to make the full Christian life a reality for all baptized peoples.

Finally, the Church community composed of laity and clergy needs to develop a greater awareness, acknowledgment, and appreciation for the diversity of the expressions of the Spirit. *Awareness* comes through experience with the range and diversity of the ever-present movement of the Spirit in all parts of the Church. In the case of the examples in this volume the diversity was both similar and different. The similarities were seen in the nearly universal response to the prompting of the Spirit to address the genuine spiritual and physical needs of local communities. The differences were evidenced in the cultural, historical, linguistic, and local circumstances of the given locations.

Acknowledgment comes with a profound humility and respect for the gifts that each Christian brings to the community. An important starting point of this acknowledgment would be seeing, looking, and viewing beyond a merely institutional and hierarchical paradigm of "perfection"—an overly stylized and "sacralized" understanding of the meaning of the Christian community—of the Church. Frequently, in the popular imagination of many, there is a skewed image of the Church, one of the Church as merely buildings and bishops. Although Christians do need a place to gather and worship as well as leaders to guide and teach them, the Church is much more than these two important structural pillars. Christians can and have gathered in a variety of settings for extended periods, and have done so without elaborate edifices and bureaucratic clerical support. Since the Church is the Body of Christ, represented in the world as a body of believers composed of laity and clergy with equal dignity and value in the eyes of God, any other ecclesial understanding that diminishes laity who are not in the "right" buildings or who do not have "proper" leaders results in merely an edificial and clerical understanding of the Church. This is a mistake because this understanding is counter-gospel; it is counter to the message of Jesus Christ.

Appreciation comes with humbly recognizing and valuing what was done with or without clergy. In the case of the examples in this book (as well as, likely, in so many other places) much was done without clergy to proclaim the gospel in season and out of season. Men and women did what the Spirit called them to do: work, labor, and suffer as well as plant and harvest the crop of the Spirit. Rather than merely being placeholders until the clergy arrived in sufficient numbers to do the "real" work of building the Church, they received, built, and maintained the faith in heroic ways. These laity were receivers of the spark, builders of the fires, and keepers of the flame. This work of the Spirit is and should be appreciated as a real movement toward the fullness of the Church community, because, as the contributors to this volume indicated, there were and are diverse ways of being the Church.

About the Contributors

Edward L. Cleary, OP, earned a PhD in social science at the University of Chicago. He published extensively on Latin American religion. Fr. Cleary has served as a priest in Bolivia and Peru, and at the time of his death in 2011 was professor of political science and the director of Latin American studies at Providence College in Rhode Island. He was also the author of *How Latin America Saved the Soul of the Catholic Church*, published by Paulist Press.

David Thomas Orique, OP, is Assistant Professor of Latin American and Iberian Atlantic World History at Providence College. Recent publications include: "Journey to the Headwaters: Bartolomé de Las Casas in a Comparative Context" (2009); "New Discoveries about an Old Manuscript: The Date, Place of Origin, and Role of the *Parecer de fray Bartolomé de las Casas* in the Making of the New Laws of the Indies" (2010). He is completing a manuscript on Las Casas's juridical approach, and is an editor for the Oxford *Handbook of Latin American Christianity*.

Bruce J. Calder is Professor of History Emeritus at the University of Illinois in Chicago. The holder of a PhD in Latin American history from the University of Texas at Austin, Dr. Calder is a recognized authority on the history of religion in Guatemala and the author of numerous writings on the history of Latin America and the Caribbean.

Cynthia Folquer, OP, is Professor of History at the Catholic University of Argentina and Director of the Institute of Historical Research at St. Thomas Aquinas North University (UNSTA), Tucumán. Her research interests include the history of Catholicism in Argentina and women and religious experience. She has organized and spoken at national and international conferences and seminars on church history and religion and has published extensively on her topics of expertise. Dr. Folquer holds a PhD in History from the University of Barcelona.

Brian J. Pierce, OP, presently resides in Rome, where he accompanies the contemplative nuns of the Order of Preachers worldwide. In the 1990s, he was part of a team of Dominicans sent to found a community of preachers in San Pedro Sula, Honduras, where they worked in the formation of lay Delegates of the Word, university students, and with men and women living with HIV-AIDS. He also spent a year ministering in a Q'eqchi indigenous parish in Guatemala. He is the author of three books, including *Martin de Porres: A Saint of the Americas* (New City Press, 2004).

Nadir Rodrigues da Silva, OP, is a member of the Congregation of the Dominican Sisters of Our Lady of the Rosary of Monteils, affiliated with the Brazilian province of Our Lady of the Rosary headquartered in São Paulo, Brazil. Between February 1978 and July 1995, she lived in Santa Fé de Goiás, a small city situated in the diocese of Goiás, whose bishop at that time was the Dominican Tomás Balduino. Today, she lives in a community in Goiânia, coordinating a center for spirituality.

Robert Schreiter, C.PP.S, is Vatican Council II Professor of Theology at the Catholic Theological Union in Chicago. He has published eighteen books in the area of inculturation, mission, world Christianity, and reconciliation. Among them are *Constructing Local Theologies, The New Catholicity: Theology between the Global and the Local, Reconciliation: Mission and Ministry in a Changing Social Order,* and *Reconciliation as Model of Mission.* He is past president of the American Society of Missiology and the Catholic Theological Society of America.